AF600042

THE JUDICIARY DEPARTMENT

OF THE

DIOCESAN CURIA

A DISSERTATION

SUBMITTED TO THE FACULTY OF THE SCHOOL OF CANON LAW OF THE CATHOLIC UNIVERSITY OF AMERICA IN PARTIAL FULFILMENT OF THE REQUIREMENTS FOR THE DEGREE OF

DOCTOR OF CANON LAW.

BY

HENRY FRANCIS DUGAN, M. A., J. C. L.,

Priest of the Diocese of Indianapolis.

THE CATHOLIC UNIVERSITY OF AMERICA

WASHINGTON, D. C.

1925

Nihil Obstat.

✠THOMAS J. SHAHAN,

Censor Deputatus.

Washingtonii, D. C., die XXIV Aprilis, 1925.

Imprimatur.

✠MICHAEL J. CURLEY,

Archiepiscopus Baltimorensis.

Baltimorae, die XXXIV Aprilis, 1925.

TABLE OF CONTENTS

CHAPTER IV.

PREFACE.

The purpose of this dissertation is to present a study of the canons in the Code of Canon Law which have reference to the diocesan curia.

This subject is a most practical one. In every diocese the ordinary must call to his assistance some of his priests. These priests form the curia of the bishop, or the diocesan curia. Through the power delegated to them by the bishop of the diocese, they give their time and attention to the many duties which are assigned to them by reason of their appointment to membership in the curia. They serve to lighten the burdens which would otherwise weigh too heavily on the ordinary of the diocese.

But one section of the curia has been selected for consideration and development in this treatise, that is, the judiciary department. This subject is treated in the Code in the Fourth Book, Canon 1572 to Canon 1593. No attempt has been made to consider the wider question of judicial procedure. The plan of the dissertation is to enumerate the list of officers who are to be found in the judicial department. A brief historical development of the office is then given and the law is quoted on such points as the power of the office under discussion, the method of appointment, and the removal from office.

The writer wishes to express his gratitude to Dr. Filippo Bernardini, J. U. D., for the advice and assistance given him in the selection of the subject of this dissertation. He also expresses his appreciation of the criticism of the work when it was in preparation. The gratitude of the writer is due to Dr. Valentine Schaaf,

O. F. M., J. D. C., and to Dr. Louis Hubert Motry, S. T. D., J. C. D., for their interest in this work, for having carefully examined the copy of this monograph and for the very helpful suggestions. He expresses his thanks to Dr. Franceso Lardone, J. U. D., the Professor of Roman Law, and to Professor de Olveira Lima, L. H. B., Professor of International Law.

THE JUDICIARY DEPARTMENT OF THE DIOCESAN CURIA.

CHAPTER I.

Definition of the Thesis.

Diocese. The term diocese signifies the territory of the churches which are subject to the jurisdiction of a bishop. In its original meaning the word meant the management of a household. This is the significance of the Greek word from which this term is derived. In the course of time this word took on a broader meaning and was used to signify the management of a city. It was soon taken into the terminology of the Romans.

The city was usually the residence of the bishop. The bishop was the leader of the faithful, the Shepherd of the flock. His duties were spread over the territory assigned to him. He managed and ruled the diocese. As the juridical territory of the city and the territory managed by the bishop were usually conterminous, the term "diocese" was soon taken into the ecclesiastical terminology. Hence the word was finally used to indicate the extent of territory under the supervision of a bishop.[1]

Curia. The curia is a collective body of officials whose duty it is to assist the ruler in the functions of government. The ruler selects the members of his curia and outlines the duties which they are to perform. Imperial Rome had its curia. It was made up of officers differing from each other in dignity and importance. Modern rulers have their specially chosen officers and secretaries. The President of the United States has his Cabinet. The members of the Cabinet are in charge of some particular branch of work in the government. They are placed in this position because they are expert in the

[1] Cath. Encyc., art. *Diocese.*

particular field of activity to which they are appointed, and in order to assist the president in the many duties which devolve upon him because of his position as head of our government.

The Supreme Pontiff has a Curia and this curia is known as the Roman Curia.[2] This body of officials in the Papal government is composed of Congregations, Tribunals, Offices and Commissions. The duties, rights and privileges of the members of the Curia are determined by the Pope, or they are determined according to the principles of the law as stated in the Code of Canon Law.[3]

Just as the Supreme Pontiff has a Curia to assist him in the rule of the Universal Church, likewise the bishop has a number of officers whose duty it is to assist the bishop in the administration of the diocese. The nature and the size of the diocesan curia is to be determined by the needs and the size of the diocese of each bishop.

History of the Curia. Maroto is of the opinion that there were no fixed or permanent offices, in the sense of a diocesan curia, until the Fourth Century. In the beginning the bishop had complete charge of his diocese. The clergy, the faithful and the possessions were under his direct rule.[4] If there was need of special help the bishop might have appointed a particular cleric to the duty. The office was discontinued when the work was completed.

With the progress of time the Church grew and flourished in accord with the plans of Her Divine Founder. She was no longer limited to a particular city or country. Her membership increased and likewise there were more priests to minister to the wants of the faithful. It was no longer possible for the bishop to give his personal attention to the many duties which came to him as head

[2] Can. 242.

[3] Can. 363.

[4] *Institutiones Juris Can.*, Tom. 11, n. 760.

of the diocese. Questions of doctrine and discipline, disputes to be settled, long journeys to be made in the interest of the Church made it necessary for the ruler of the diocese to call to his assistance competent priests. The curia is the result of a natural growth and evolution. The bishop formed the first curia, sharing his jurisdiction to the extent necessary for this help. The bishop appointed the officer and consequently he had the right to discontinue the services of the officer, and abolish the office when there was no longer need of the service in question.

The mention of a few of the early diocesan officials will help in comparing the present curia with the curia of former times. The Archpriest held a very important position. He was selected to look after the interests of the priests of the diocese, when the bishop was absent from his diocese. He celebrated the Holy Sacrifice in the principal, or the Cathedral Church. The Archdeacon was selected by the bishop to assist in the administration of the temporalities of the diocese. He was permitted to conduct a visitation of the parishes. He investigated abuses and at times acted in the role of judge, settling disputes and punishing crimes. The Econom was known in the Western Church as the Vicedominus. He was charged with the temporal affairs of the diocese, such as land and property and he could dispose of these. The Advocates or the Defensores, were appointed to safeguard the rights of the Church before the courts. They defended ecclesiastical causes before the civil magistrates. The Notaries were commissioned to present a written account of the ecclesiastical proceedings and to keep a record of all ecclesiastical documents such as letters of request, dispensations granted and other similar papers. The Archivist, the Chancellor and the Librarian were those officers whose duty it was to keep in order and to preserve all these documents. The official Interpreter or Expositor was assigned to the important duty of translating and explaining the text of Sacred Scripture to the faithful. The Catechists instructed the faithful in the rudiments of the Faith. The Grand Penitentiary acted in the capacity of the official confessor for the faithful. The Chanters or the Cantores were appointed to render the approved chant of the Church at all liturgical functions. Besides these there were others of minor importance who assisted the bishop in looking after the affairs of the diocese. Laymen could have been chosen for some of the offices, such as the Advocates, but it seems that the more common practise was to appoint clerics.

These various offices were not established at one and the same time. The offices were created and the appointments made to the office in accord with the needs of the diocese. When it was necessary for the bishop to be absent from his diocese, the Archpriest was appointed to have charge of the clergy of the diocese. When the bishop was within his proper territory the burdens were many and these he shared with the priests whom he had honored by a call to the duties of the curia. It is to be noted that the offices of the curia which have been mentioned are somewhat different from the offices existing in the curia of the dioceses today. The reason for this is evident. The bishop instituted certain official positions which were needed at a particular time. The need no longer existing, the bishop discontinued the service of the cleric when his services were no longer necessary to the bishop. With the same authority, the bishop made new appointments to answer new needs. This accounts for the change in the personnel of the curia. Changes in the future will be fewer, however, since the Code gives special consideration to the officers which should make up the diocesan curia of today.[5]

The Judiciary Power in the Diocesan Curia. The members of the diocesan curia are dependent upon the bishop for the jurisdiction which they exercise as members of the official family. This jurisdiction varies in

[5] C. I. C., Bk. II, Tit. VIII, C. IV.

nature and extent. The bishop is limited in conferring of jurisdiction only when such limitations are clearly expressed in the Canons of the Code.[6] The jurisdiction of the vicar general and his relation to the bishop, the jurisdiction of the Official, or the Judge, in the curia of the bishop are points which are clearly defined in the Code. In such matters the bishop will follow the law as stated in the Code of Canon Law.[7]

Division of Jurisdiction. There are two kinds of jurisdiction. Jurisdiction may be either voluntary or contentious.[8] This distinction applies also to the jurisdiction delegated to the members of the bishop's curia. The officers in the curia who act in virtue of the former are limited to such duties which are of a secretarial or administrative nature. This may include official correspondence such as Chancery notices or announcements which the bishop sends to his priests through the Chancery. It may be the sending out of the official notice that the bishop has granted a dispensation which was requested. Those who are connected with the diocesan Archives act in the same capacity. The office of Chancellor of the diocese is an example of the voluntary form of jurisdiction.[9] He is the official secretary of the bishop and his communications concerning diocesan affairs are always conducted in the name of, and with the authorization of, the Ordinary.

Contentious jurisdiction implies the exercise of an authority which is quite different. It empowers the one on whom it is conferred to act in an executive, legislative, or judicial capacity. The person so delegated may act in the role of a judge. He thereby has the power to read the law officially. As a judge, he may hold court, hear causes, interpret the law, render decisions, and fix the

[6] Can. 363.

[7] Bouix, *Tract. de Judiciis,* Pars II, Sec. III.

[8] Bouix, *o. c., l. c.*

[9] Wernz, *Jus Decr.,* V. II, n. 633.

penalty for misdeeds. The judicial aspect of the curial activity is the matter to be considered in the present treatise. The meaning and the purpose of this power will be shown. The great importance of such power in a society will then be deduced from this as a natural conclusion.

Meaning and the Purpose of the Judicial Power. It is not within the scope of the title of this dissertation to give proof of the foundation of the Catholic Church as a perfect society. This will be understood as an established fact. A doubt in any critical mind can be very easily dispelled by the most passing observation of the activity of the Church. The Catholic Church is a great force in the world today, influencing the minds, hearts, and the lives of men. With a well-defined code of doctrine and morals, her activity in all the problems which are vexing society today, She is giving undeniable evidence of her life as an active organized society.

Being a well-organized society She must possess all the prerogatives to be found in a society perfectly organized. She must possess, and She must be able to use, all those powers which make of an aggregation of human beings a society, or a unit. It is the prudent use of these powers that will make of the many individual human beings, a moral unit, agreed on the accomplishment of a common purpose. These powers are the executive, the legislative and the judicial powers.

Executive Power. There must be in the Church a Chief Executive to direct and formulate the policy to be followed by those who are the members of this society. The Pope of Rome is the visible Head of the Church. He is the earthly representative of Christ, the Divine Founder of the Church. The Supreme Pontiff is the successor of St. Peter, the first Pope, who held his office by a direct appointment from Jesus Christ. The Pope is assisted in the government of the Church by the Bishops who are appointed from Rome.

Legislative Power. Laws and regulations are necessary for the preservation of moral unity in any group of individuals. The Decalogue is the basis of all legislation in the Church. This is the legislation which represents a direct revelation from Almighty God. There are other laws, which the Church, guided by Divine Wisdom, has found necessary to enact. These laws may by purely ecclesiastical, such as the diocesan regulations concerning clerical dress and social life. They may be ecclesiastical laws based on the divine or natural law, for example, the precept to hear Mass on Sunday, the regulations on fasting and abstinence, the duties of the married state and many other such laws. Regardless of what their foundation may be, it is sufficient for the faithful to know that the law issues from the legislative authority in the Church.

Judicial Power. From the executive and the legislative authority a third power follows necessarily. This power is the judicial power. It pertains to the administration of justice. The judicial power calls for the existence of judges and courts. The judicial procedure is concerned with the actions of the members of a society to decide whether or not the actions are in conformity with the statutes of the law. A law may be negative or positive. It may command the performance of a certain act. An unlawful action is one which is contrary to a law. The decision as to the lawfulness or the unlawfulness of an act comes within the scope of the judicial power. In the court of a society the guilt or the innocence of the individual member is established. The judge presides over the department of the judiciary. He is the official interpreter of the law and his jurisdiction extends to all those causes which come within the limits of his power. This official position of the judge to interpret the law renders the individual estimates and individual interpretations of what a law may mean useless and unnecessary. The decision of the judge applies the law to the case. Unless there be just cause for a recourse to another court or a legal reason for appeal to a higher court, the decision of the first instance stands and the case is closed.

Importance of Judicial Power. The great importance of the judicial power in any society is apparent. What is the benefit of a code of laws to a society unless the laws have some influence on the daily lives of the members of that society? Why have fixed statutes if the individual members of the society be permitted to disregard them at will? Of what benefit can a law be to a society, if the law may be disobeyed without fear of punishment? These questions were surely in the mind of Pope John XXII when he wrote: "It would be folly to make laws unless there were some one to enforce them."[10] This important power of enforcing laws, is vested in the courts and operates through the decisions of the judges. In the courts of justice the guilty receive the punishment for their transgressions of the law, and the innocent are declared free through the impartial adjudication of their acts. This judicial institution, like so many other institutions in the social life, had its beginning, and developed according to the needs of the society whose needs it served.

Personnel of the Diocesan Judiciary. The persons to be considered in this dissertation are those members of the diocesan curia who attend to the "res judiciales." It is quite clear from the Code that the fullness of the judiciary power is vested in the Ordinary of the diocese. This fact is established from Canon 1572, § 1:

> "In unaquaque diocesi et pro omnibus causis a iure non expresse exceptis, iudex primae instantiae est loci Ordinarius, qui iudiciariam potestatem exercere potest, per se vel per alios, secundum canones qui sequuntur."

The canon states that this is true in every diocese, "in unaquaque diocesi." Ecclesiastical territory which has

[10] *Cap. un, de Judiciis,* II. I, in Extrav. Comm.

been canonically erected constitutes a diocese.[11] Both an abbacy and a prelacy *nullius* are included in the term diocese.[12] The Apostolic Vicariate and the Apostolic Prefecture are not to be included.[13] Should it happen that the episcopal see be vacant by death or other reason, the judiciary power is then held by the vicar capitular, or, as in this country, by the administrator of the diocese. It follows logically, that the judiciary power is also enjoyed by the one who rules an abbacy or prelacy *nullius*.[14]

The Ordinary may exercise this power in person, "per se" or he may act through another, "per alios." This power is ordinary and permanent as in the case of the officialis of the curia, or it is merely delegated for a particular time and cause as it is done when the synodal judges act.[15] When reference is made to the personnel of the judiciary in this chapter there is no intention of including the Ordinary of the diocese. On the contrary, those to whom the Ordinary has delegated this power are meant. The following quotation from the Code will demonstrate who these persons are:

"Curia diocesana constat illis personis quae Episcopo aliive, qui loco Episcopi, diocesim regit, opem praestant in regimine totius diocesis. Quare ad eam pertinent vicarius generalis, officialis, cancellarius, promotor justitiae, defensor vinculi, synodales iudices et examinatores, parochi consultores, auditores, notarii, cursores et apparitores." [16]

In the reading of this canon it is well to keep in mind what has been stated concerning the extension of the term diocese in Canon Law. The same statement applies to the term Ordinary. The diocesan curia is composed of the persons who assist the bishop in the duties of governing the diocese. This group is composed of both

[11] Noval, Lib. IV, *De Processibus*, n. 110.

[12] Can. 215.

[13] Noval, *o. c., l. c.*

[14] Can. 215.

[15] S. d'Angelo, *La Curia Diocesana*, Sez. II, Cap. I, n. 6.

[16] Can. 363, par. 1 and 2.

lay and clerical agents.[17] The extent to which they may assist the Ordinary depends entirely upon the nature of the office to which they are appointed. The curators and the apparitors,[18] by the material aid they give, are truly members of the curia, as well as the vicar general, or the official of the diocese.

The officers of the curia mentioned in Canon 363, the second paragraph, may be divided into two classes. The basis of the distinction is the nature of the jurisdiction which the bishop confers upon them. To the first group are assigned all those who assist in the administration of the spiritual and temporal matters in the diocese. These persons have voluntary jurisdiction and among them we find the vicar general, chancellor, parish consultors, etc.[19] To the second group belong the other members of the curia and their duties center about the judicial affairs, or the "*causae contentiosae*" of the diocese. To this group the bishop grants jurisdiction over criminal and contentious causes which may arise.[20] The purpose of this dissertation is to consider the canonical powers of this second group. Hence the official,[21] synodal judges,[22] instructors and counsellors,[23] notaries, the promotor of justice, defender of the bond,[24] cursors and apparitors,[25] will be considered historically and canonically in the chapters which follow. Before taking up the first of these, the official, an historical sketch will be given of the archdeacon and also of the vicar general. The former deserves our attention because of his precedence in history as an important officer in the curia. The latter is to be considered because of the relation between the archdeacon and the vicar general and more especially because of the provision in the Code which makes it possible for the vicar general to act in the capacity of official or judge as well, in the diocesan curia.[26]

[17] Can. 373, *par. I.*

[18] Can. 1591, *par. I.*

[19] Vermeersch-Creusen, *Epitome Iuris Canonici*, Tom. I, n. 432.

[20] Vermeersch-Creusen, *o. c., l. c.*

[21] Can. 1572.

[22] Can. 1574.

[23] Can. 1580.

[24] Can. 1585-1590.

[25] Can. 1591-1593.

[26] Can. 1573, *par. I.*

CHAPTER II.

Important Officers in the Early Curia.

Curia a Necessity. The rapid growth of the Church and the consequent multiplication of the duties which fell to the lot of the bishops, are the reasons given by Canonists for the organization of the diocesan curia.[1] Among the first diocesan officers, the Archdeacon stands out as one of the important members of the curia. His prominence is noted as early as the fourth century.[2] The first mark of distinction which characterized the Archdeacon was that of priority or presidency over seven deacons. It seems that the custom of Apostolic times of appointing deacons was continued in some of the ancient Churches.[3] The appointment of one of the deacons to be the Archdeacon was made by the bishops. The one appointed was not necessarily the senior deacon but one whom the bishops considered qualified for this position.[4]

The Archdeacon.

The principal work of the Archdeacon was the custody and administration of the temporal goods of the diocese. He was the one to whom the offerings of the faithful were entrusted. With the money entrusted to him he helped the poor and those in need of assistance. He was present and assisted the bishop at the ceremony of ordination. He exercised jurisdiction over clerics who were his subjects. He was empowered to visit the parishes, point out and correct abuses which he found. He might do this by a judicial procedure in which process the Archdeacon acted as judge.[5]

[1] Wernz, *Jus Canonicum*, Tom. II, Tit VIII, Art. I, n. 634.

[2] Thomassin, *Vetus et Nova Eccl. Discip.*, Cap. XVII, P. 1. 12.

[3] Wernz, *o. c.*, *l. c.*

[4] Thomassin, *o. c.*, P. I, l. 2, Cap. 17, n. 11.

[5] C. 1, par. 11 D. 25; Cap. 1, 2, 3, X, de off. archid., I, 23.

The foregoing applies to the person and the activity of the Archdeacon who resided in the episcopal city. He was called the "Archidiaconus Civitatis," that is, of the city, in contradistinction to the rural archdeacon.[6]

The Rural Archdeacon. The rural Archdeacon was appointed to a certain locality of the diocese. This place was known as the Archdeanery and was precided over by the Archdeacon. The practise of dividing the diocese into archdeaneries is found in France at the beginning of the ninth century.[7] According to Fournier, "There were three archdeacons in the diocese of Paris, six in the diocese of Chartres and two in Arran. In former times there was but one."[8] Sometime after the ninth century this custom was gradually introduced in England, Germany and later into Italy.[9]

In the eleventh century new powers were assumed by the Archdeacon. By this time he claimed and made use of, juridical as well as administratorial power. In the archdeanery, the Archdeacon considered himself supreme. In disputes, legal controversies and the punishment of crime, the Archdeacon acted in the role of a judge. His tribunal was the court of first instance. From this court an appeal could be made to the episcopal tribunal, or that tribunal in which the bishop was judge.[10]

At the close of the twelfth and in the early part of the thirteenth, the bishops faced a serious problem. The Archdeacon was exceeding the rightful powers of his office. He was assuming a priority in ecclesiastical legal procedure which belonged to the bishop of the diocese. Because of this condition it became necessary to define the limits and nature of the Archdeacon's jurisdiction, for the safeguarding of the episcopal authority and dignity.[11]

[6] Wernz, *o. c., l. c.*, II.

[7] Fournier, *Les Origines du Vicaire Général*, Chap. III.

[8] Fournier, *ibid.*

[9] Wernz, *o. c., ibid.*

[10] Cap. 7, 9, 10, X, *de off. archid.*, I, 23.

[11] Cap. 6, 8, X, *de off. archid.;* Cap. 3, X, *de poenis*, V, 37.

The situation was further aggravated by the change which had crept in gradually in the method of appointment of the Archdeacons. Formerly, the Archdeacon was appointed by the bishop who was free to make the selection. The evils which accompanied the practise of conferring of benefices were felt here also. The archdeanery was a benefice and desired because of the rank of position and income. The civil authorities often interfered in the appointments. In some instances the civil ruler made the appointment directly. Again he might influence the choice of the bishop. The Cathedral Chapter had been known to select an Archdeacon, independent of the bishop's wish in the matter.[12]

The inevitable consequence of this interference was that the Archdeacons appointed by authority other than episcopal, considered themselves independent of the Ordinary of the diocese in matters of administration and jurisdiction. As Maroto states, these officers considered their position "a jure" that is, by right or by law. It is clear from this that the bishop might experience some difficulty in the removal of an Archdeacon who had exceeded the limits of the archdeaconal power.[13]

Legislation. "It is not to be wondered at," writes Wernz, " that the bishops took council as to the method and means by which they might limit and control the powers of the Archdeacon, and to appoint other officials in curia whose appointment and removal depended upon the Ordinary." [14]

The first effort to correct the abuse was the appointment of a new type of officer in the curia. There is record of this action early in the twelfth century.[15] In the thirteenth century the bishops appointed officers who were to take their place in curia residing in the city with the bishop, or to live at a stated place in the diocese.

[12] Maroto, *o. c.*, Tom. II, n. 760.

[13] Maroto, *o. c.*, *l. c.*, " a jure datur, non ab episcopo assumptus."

[14] Wernz, *o. c.*, *l. c.*, c. 8, Conc. Turon., 1234.

[15] Wernz, *o. c.*, *l. c.;* c. 22, Conc. Rothomag. 1190.

These officers were appointed by the bishops and were removable from office "ad nutum episcopi." The official who resided in the city was called the "officialis principalis" and to him appeal could be made from the court of the "officiales foranei" or those who were appointed in certain parts of the diocese, outside of the cathedral city.[16]

It is the opinion of Wernz that the "officialis principalis " is the vicar general of later history. This officer, the vicar general, is mentioned in the Decretals of Gregory IX. In the later compilation of Boniface VI and Clement, the office of vicar general frequently referred to in the constitution of laws and regulations concerning the position and activity of the vicar general in the curia.[17] Although this office was not instituted in the thirteenth century it is between the years 1234 and 1298 that this official institution became known. This same period marks the decline of the Archdeacon's powers and importance.

In the Council of Trent. The bishops met the problem of the Archdeacon's power in another way, that is, by direct legislation against them. In the Council of Trent, it was declared that the Archdeacon could not act as a judge in *prima instantia* in matrimonial cases. He was also forbidden to render judgment in criminal cases involving the trial of clerics.[18] In a later session of the council they declared that the Archdeacon had no jurisdiction over cases of clerics charged with the crime of concubinage. Neither could the Archdeacon excommunicate those against whom a charge had been made.[19]

By enactments such as those just cited, as well as through the more direct procedure of the bishops in appointing new officers, the archdeacon lost his position and powers in the curia of the diocese. Today he is not

[16] Wernz, *o. c.*, *l. c.*, quoting Inn. IV, in Const. " Romana Ecclesia."

[17] Cap. 23, *de off. vic.*, I, 13, in Sext; Cap. 2, de rescr. 1, 2 in Clem.

[18] Sess. XXIV, de ref., C. 20.

[19] Sess. XXV, de ref., Cap. 3.

mentioned in the list of the diocesan officers. The title of Archdeacon today is more commonly known in the liturgical and ceremonial functions than in the juridical offices of the Church.

A phase, somewhat different from the official character of the Archdeacon, his decline, removal, etc. from the curia is presented in a late work of Edouard Fournier, "Les Origines du Vicaire General."[20] This work is an historico-canonical study of the origin of the vicar general as an ecclesiastical officer. Fournier objects to the statement that the office of vicar general was created by the bishops for the express purpose of suppressing the Archdeacon.[21] He tries to establish the point that the official appointed about the eleventh century in France is an officer quite different and distinct in his activities from the vicar general of a later century.[22] More attention will be given to this particular point in a later chapter of this dissertation.

Fournier's Opinion. It is the opinion of Fournier that the historical development of the office of vicar general should be traced from another ecclesiastical officer—the procurator-general. This officer seems to have originated about the thirteenth century. The French Canonist quotes and adopts Reiffenstuel's definition of a procurator, that is one who is "pro alio curator, nempe prodomino, cujus loco et nomine res seu negotio . . . sua gerit et administrat."[23] According to this definition, a procurator to represent him. If a Bishop were preadministers the affairs of another person, many instances are quoted to show how frequently procurators were used during the Middle Ages. Thus the parish priest who could not attend the diocesan synod appointed a procurator to represent him. If a bishop were prevented from attending the provincial council he appointed his procurator as his representative. A quotation from the Decretals of Pope Gregory IX shows that

[20] Paris, 1922.

[21] Chap. II.

[22] Chap. IV.

[23] Fournier, Chap. V, p. 73.

Pope Alexander III addressed a rescript to the "procuratori et canonicis Sorranis." [24] This procurator, Fournier explains, is evidently, from the sense of the context, an administrator of the diocese of Sorro, whose bishop is dead. It is in this type of officer in ecclesiastical procedure that Fournier sees the forerunner of the vicar general, who is a prominent officer of the diocesan curia according to the present legislation of the Code.

Wernz and Fournier. Both Wernz and Fournier agree as to the main facts in the discussion. The archdeacon gradually lost his power and position as a diocesan official. The Council of Trent, though eulogizing the merits of the archdeacons, reduced their position from one of juridical importance to that of a mere titular dignitary in the episcopal family. Both authors agree as to the fact that a new office was created, to which office was gradually ceded the power formerly granted to the archdeacon. This officer of later appointment became the administrator of the diocese. The disagreement in the discussion seems to arise over the motive which animated the change in the policy. Wernz follows the traditional statement of historians, that the vicar general was created for the express purpose of dethroning the unruly archdeacons. Fournier terms this an undignified and unworthy motive to attribute to the hierarchy in attempting to meet a crisis. Though Wernz [25] recognizes and quotes the work of Fournier he does not openly agree or disagree. Hence it seems that the question still remains one open for discussion for the writers and students of history, and as an open question we leave it.

With this somewhat brief review of the history of the archdeacon and vicar general, some ideas are now in the mind concerning the juridical position of these officials in former centuries. The logical step now is to take up the consideration of the present status of the vicar gen-

[24] C. IV, 1; X, 17.

[25] Wernz, *o. c.*, footnote, p. 673.

eral. A presentation of the Canons from the Code will give the proper aspect of this question.

The Vicar General.

Can. 366. § 1. **"Quoties rectum diocesis regimen id exigat, constituendus est ab Episcopo Vicarius Generalis, qui ipsum potestate ordinaria in toto territorio adiuvet.**

§ 2. **Vicarius Generalis libere ab Episcopo designatur, qui eum potest ad nutum removere.**

§ 3. **Unus tantum constituatur, nisi vel rituum diversitas vel amplitudo diocesis aliud exigat; sed, Vicario Generali absente vel impedito, Episcopus alium constituere potest qui eius vices suppleat."**

There are three important points contained in the first paragraph of this Canon, which are: (1) the reason why a vicar general should be appointed; (2) nature of the power conferred on the vicar general; and (3) the person having the right to make the appointment.

The vicar general is a priest lawfully appointed by the bishop, empowered to exercise the episcopal jurisdiction in any part of the diocese. He acts by authorization of the Bishop, so that the bishop is responsible for the legal acts of his vicar.[26]

Reason for the Appointment. The reason for the appointment of this vicar is the "rectum regimen diocesis" the proper conduct of diocesan administration. The size of the diocese, in extent and numbers, the spiritual and material affairs demanding attention, and the activity of the bishops, are a few of the circumstances which will determine the question in regard to the need of a vicar general.

Appointment to come from the Bishop. The bishop is the one who appoints the diocesan vicar general. An abbot or a prelate *nullius* may also appoint a vicar gen-

[26] Vermeersch-Creusen, Tom. I, n. 433.

eral if one be necessary in the territory which they rule.[26a] Vicars and Prefects Apostolic do not enjoy this right under the general law. Benedict XIV in the Constitution "Quam sublimi," 1745, granted to Vicars and Prefects Apostolic the privilege of appointing a vicar delegate.[27] The competence of this officer is similar to the jurisdiction conferred on the vicar general by the Code.[28]

The obligation of appointing a Vicar General is not absolute. The decision as to when it is necessary is left to the judgment of the bishop. Should a bishop, through negligence, fail to meet the need, the Holy See may interfere and appoint the vicar general. A vicar general so appointed is not removable *ad nutum episcopi.*[29]

Power Conferred. The third point to be noted in this paragraph is the nature of the power conferred on the vicar general is ordinary power throughout the diocese. It is ordinary because it is conferred by the Code, the general law, and "vi officii," that is, by reason of the appointment to the office. This ordinary jurisdiction is however a vicariate power since he acts in the name of the Ordinary. The Ordinary is responsible for the legal acts of the vicar.[30] It is clearly stated in this paragraph (Can. 366, § 1) that the jurisdiction of the vicar general is coextensive with the territorial limits of the diocese.

It is the Ordinary of the diocese who has the right to make the appointment. He is independent of all powers —both temporal and ecclesiastical. Neither the civil authorities nor the cathedral chapter nor the consultors, may lawfully interfere. The bishop may use his own discretion in considering the removal of the vicar general. He may be removed from office whenever the bishop finds it advisable to remove him.

[26a] Can. 323, § 3.

[27] Const. "Quam sublimi," 1745.

[28] Wernz, *o. c.*, 636 (AAS. XII, 1920, p. 120); Ver.-Cr., p. 254.

[29] Wernz, *o. c.*, quoting Ferraris, n. 636.

[30] D'Angelo, *o. c.*, p. 10, n. 4.

The Number of Vicars General. The Code recognizes two possibilities, when either one existing, the bishop may appoint more than one vicar general. In the year 1742 Pope Benedict XIV had conceded the privilege to the bishops to have more than one vicar general in those dioceses where there were a considerable number of the faithful of different rites, for example, Greeks, Ruthenians and Latins in the same diocese.[31] This point is mentioned in the Code, "rituum diversitas," hence it has the force of general law.[32] The second possibility is the consideration of the size of the diocese. A densely populated diocese or a diocese covering an extensive territory may be sufficient reason for the appointment of more than one vicar general.[33]

Requisite Qualifications. The vicar general of the diocese should be a man chosen from the ranks of the secular clergy. He should be at least thirty years old. The Code requires that the appointee be one who has the degree of doctor or licentiate in theology and canon law, or at least one who is proficient in these branches. His mental and moral qualifications should be the highest, and his ability and prudence should be evident from his past activity in the diocese.[34]

If the Holy See appoints a religious community to take charge of a diocese, the vicar general of that diocese may be a priest of that community.[35] The mere fact that a religious is made the head of a diocese does not indicate that the community has been appointed over the diocese. If the *community* is to be in charge of the diocese the appointment will be made to the community as such. No example of this is to be found in our own country.

Paragraph three of Canon 367 enumerates those who are excluded from the office of vicar general.

1. The Canonical penitentiary.

[31] *Etsi Pastoralis,* May 28, 1742.

[32] Can. 366, § 3.

[33] Can. 366, § 3.

[34] Can. 367, § 1, § 3.

[35] Can. 367, § 2.

2. Blood relations of the Ordinary in the first degree or the second mixed with the first.
3. Parish priests and those engaged in the cura animarum.

The Ordinary is forbidden to appoint blood relations in the degree mentioned above, lest his motives be questioned. He may not appoint a brother, neither his nephew. The penitentiary and the parish priest and those entrusted with the care of souls are excluded lest in the external forum they be forced to deal with subjects over whom they have power in the internal forum. The jurisdiction of the vicar general is in externo and he should never be suspected of acting in external forum on matters submitted to him in the confessional.

Power of the Vicar General. The vicar general, " vi-officii," by reason of appointment to the office, possesses ordinary proper jurisdiction in every part of the diocese.[36] The right to exercise this jurisdiction begins when he takes possession of the office.[36] The jurisdiction extends to both spiritual and *temporal* affairs in the diocese.

The two exceptions in Canon 368 limit the power of the vicar general. He has no jurisdiction in those matters which the bishop may reserve to himself.[38] How far may the bishop go in limiting the power of the vicar general by reservations? D'Angelo is of the opinion that the bishop may not go to such extremes in limiting the power of the vicar general as to change the nature of the universality of jurisdiction. This universality of power as to persons and territory, is granted to the vicar general by the general law according to the Canons of the Code. Should the reservations be too numerous and the vicar general be compelled to seek special concessions from the bishop, the character of a vicar general

[36] Can. 368, § 1; Can. 197; Can. 198.

[37] Can. 1095, § 1, n. 1.

[38] Can. 368, § 1.

would be destroyed and instead there would be merely a delegated agent.[39]

Limitation of Power. The jurisdiction of the vicar general is limited when the General law, the Code, requires a special commission from the bishop for certain functions. The acts which may not be executed by a vicar general except by special commissions are:

(1) The institution of ecclesiastical offices.[40]
(2) The calling, or presiding over a diocesan synod.[41]
(3) The appointing of pastors.[42]
(4) The removal of assistants, "vicars" in parishes.[43]
(5) The organization of pious associations.[44]
(6) The reservation of sins.[45]
(7) The concession of dismissorial letters.[46]
(8) The grant of permission for a "matrimonium conscientiae." [74]
(9) The consecration of a church or place of worship.[48]
(10) The grant of permission for building a church.[49]
(11) The authentication of relics.[50]
(12) The regulation of the amount of a stipend.[51]
(13) The establishment of a benefice.[52]
(14) The union or conferring of benefices.[53]
(15) The grant of a canonical institution.[54]
(16) The permission for the exchange of benefices.[55]
(17) The fixing ("statuere") of ecclesiastical punishments.[56]
(18) The vicar general is excluded from the whole of the second part of Book Four of the Code.[57]

[39] D'Angelo, *o. c.*, p. 15.
[40] Can. 152.
[41] Can. 357, § 1.
[42] Can. 455, § 1.
[43] Can. 477, § 1.
[44] Can. 686, § 4.
[45] Can. 893, § 1.
[46] Can. 958, § 1; Can. 959.
[47] Can. 1104.
[48] Can. 1155, § 1.
[49] Can. 1162, § 1.
[50] Can. 1283, § 2.
[51] Can. 1303, § 3.
[52] Can. 1414, § 3.
[53] Can. 1423, § 1; Can. 1432, § 2.
[54] Can. 1466, § 2.
[55] Can. 1487, § 1.
[56] Can. 2220, § 2.
[57] Can. 2002.

(19) The absolution *in foro externo* of heretics, apostates, etc., from excommunication.[58]

The Mandatum Speciale. There is a dispute among canonists as to the time when the "mandatum speciale," the special commission which the Code requires, should be given. Should the bishop delegate in each particular case when the Code so requires, for example, at the time of the consecration of a particular church? Can this concession be made in a more general way, say at the time the vicar general is appointed—giving him jurisdiction for all matters—"etiam quoad omnia quae speciale mandatum requirunt"—? Oietti seems to favor a general delegation covering all cases. He styles it a "mandatum speciale permanens." [59] Badii does not favor the concession by a general formula to cover any and all cases which may arise in the future.[60] Vermeersch holds that the "mandatum speciale" may be granted by way of a general delegation. He says: "Episcopus potest ipsis litteris, quibus vicarium generalem, constituit, addere se eum deputare—" etiam ad omnia quae speciale mandatum requirunt." This seems to be a safe and satisfactory statement on the question. The preceding paragraphs contain the present legislation as to what functions require this special delegation.[61]

Canon 2002 limits the power of the vicar general by forbidding him to act in the cause of a beatification or a canonization of a servant of God. This canon states that the vicar general is not to be understood in that section of the Code which deals with processes and persons involved in beatifications, etc., when the name Ordinary occurs. This, of course, is an express exception to Canon 198.

The vicar general is declared ineligible for appointment to office on the committees selected by the Bishop

[58] Can. 2314, § 2.

[59] Quoted by D'Angelo, *o. c.*, p. 17.

[60] Badii, *Inst. I. Can.*, p. 220.

[61] Vermeersch-Creusen, *o. c.*, Tom. I, n. 436.

for the consideration of disciplinary or administrative questions in the diocese or seminary.[62]

The vicar general may execute Apostolic rescripts which may have been sent to the bishop of the diocese if there be no restriction to the contrary. The common or habitual faculties which the Holy See grants to the bishop, belong to the vicar general also.[63]

The vicar general, being the vicar of the Ordinary of the diocese, must keep in mind the principle that he acts in the name of the bishop. Hence the bishop should be consulted on the important acts of the curia which are directed toward the discipline of the clergy or the laity.[64] "Let him beware," warns the Code, "lest he use his powers contrary to the mind and will of the bishop. having due regard for the prescriptions of Canon 44." There is no appeal from the vicar general to the bishop.[65] A faculty denied by the vicar general may be conceded by the bishop, the fact being mentioned that the vicar general had refused to grant petition.[66]

Right to Recognition as Prelate. Canon 370, §1:

"Praesente etiam episcopo, vicarius generalis publice privatimque praecedentiae ius habet super omnibus diocesis clericis, non exclusis dignitatibus et canonicis ecclesiae cathedralis, etiam in choro et actibus et capitularibus, nisi clericus charactere episcopoli praefulgeat, et vicarius generalis eodem careat.

§ 2. **"Si vicarius generalis sit episcopus, omnia honorifica privilegia episcoporum titularium obtinet; secus durante munere habet tantum privilegia et insignia Protonotarii apostolici titularis."**

In the first paragraph of this canon the precedence of the vicar general is declared. In the presence of the bishop, the vicar general takes precedence over all diocesan clerics, including dignitaries, prelates and the canons of the cathedral chapter. Should there be a cleric

[62] Can. 1359, § 1 and § 2.

[63] Can. 66; Can. 198, § 1.

[64] Can. 369.

[65] Ver.-Creus., *o. c.*, n. 438.

[66] Can. 399; Can. 44.

in the diocese raised to the episcopate, he alone will take precedence over the vicar general if the vicar be not a member of the episcopate.

It is now the general law that if the vicar be a bishop, he may avail himself of all the honorary privileges of a titular bishop. Such would be the case if the auxiliary bishop of the diocese be the vicar general. If the vicar be not a bishop, the Code prescribes that he is to have all the privileges and insignia of a titular prothonotary apostolic prelate during the time he holds this office in the diocesan curia. The last clause of the second paragraph of this canon is based on the Motu Proprio of Pope Pius X, "Inter multiplices," Feb. 21, 1905.[67]

The Expiration of this Office. Canon 371:

"Expirat vicarii generalis iurisdictio per ipsius renuntiationem ad normam can. 183-191, aut revocationem ei ab Episcopo intimatam, aut sedis episcopalis vacationem; suspenditur vero suspensa episcopali iurisdictione."

In this canon the Code defines the manner in which the office of vicar general expires or is suspended. Some of these follow the general law on loss of ecclesiatical office; the others are peculiar to the office of the vicar general.

1. The ordinary and more common way by which an ecclesiastical office ceases is by *resignation.*[68] The Canons referred to to which govern the process of resignation of an ecclesiastical office state that the resignation should be for a just reason,[69] there being no special prohibition preventing the resignation. The resignation must be a free act, not the result of fear, threat or violence.[70] The legal formalities are to be observed, hence either in writing, or if oral, before two witnesses.[71] Finally, the resignation must be accepted by the lawful superior.[72]

[67] D'Angelo, *o. c.*, p. 23.

[68] Can. 183.

[69] Can. 184.

[70] Can. 185.

[71] Can. 186.

[72] Can. 187.

2. This office may cease by *revocation.* This revocation or recall must come from the Ordinary. The vicar is to be duly notified of the will of his superior in recalling the appointment.

3. The *death, removal* or the *resignation* of the bishop signifies the cessation of the office of the vicar general of that diocese. From this it follows that the jurisdiction of the vicar general is dependent upon the continued and uninterrupted jurisdiction of the bishop of the diocese.[73]

Canon 430 considers the case of a bishop being removed from one diocese to another. Even though he were to remain in the diocese "a quo" as Apostolic Administrator of that diocese during the allotted space of time of four months, the vicar general in the diocese "a quo" would cease to function on the day of the notification of the transfer.[74]

[73] D'Angelo, *o. c.*, p. 26.

[74] Can. 430, § 2, § 3, no. 1.

CHAPTER III.

The Officialis.

The Judge. The Code states that it is the duty of every Bishop to appoint a judge as one of the members of the diocesan curia. This judge is called the officialis and the method of appointment, competency, qualification, and other related questions are outlined in Canon 1573. A judge in the legal sense is a judicial officer appointed or elected to preside in the courts of law and to decide legal questions duly brought before him. The judge presides over the judiciary department, and it is through this department that laws are administered.[1]

History. In ancient Roman law there were two phases observed in judicial procedure. The contention, or crime was first brought to the notice of the Roman magistrate or ruler. He did not investigate the facts of the case but decided it to be a case within the scope of the law and appointed the judge, giving him the necessary instructions. The process which was conducted by the magistrate was known as "in jure," or in the law. The investigation proper before the judge was termed "in judicio," or the judgment of the cause.[2]

Pretor—Judex in Roman Law. The Roman pretor was a civil magistrate who had charge of the administration of justice. The first pretor was appointed in the year 366 B. C.[3]

According to Livy the chief functions of the pretorship were "jus in urbe dicere," to interpret the law officially,[4] at times they commanded the armies of the state, and even supplied in the absence of the consuls within the limits of the city.[5]

[1] Funk and Wagnalls, Dict.—" judge "—" judiciary."

[2] Smith, *Dictionary of Greek Antiquities*, v, " iudex."

[3] Smith, *o. c.*, Ledlie, *The Institutes by Sohm.*, par. 57.

[4] Livy, VI, 42.

[5] Smith, *o. c.*

Another pretor, the Pretor Peregrinus, was appointed in the year 246 B. C. The duty of this officer was to administer justice in disputed matters between the peregrini, the travellers in Rome, or between peregrini and Roman citizens.[6] The other pretor was then known as the Pretor Urbanus and his duties were within the city of Rome.

The pretors existed in varying numbers in the period of Justinian Law, in the latter days of the Empire and continued to exercise jurisdiction in judicial matters.[7]

Legislative and Judicial Power of Apostolic Times. Christ, the Divine Founder of the Church, appointed His Chief Executive, St. Peter. The one appointed by Christ to be the representative head of the Church, received his commission before the day of the Ascension. This commission carried with it all the power necessary for the conduct of the affairs of the Church.[8] St. John is the witness of the conferring of this commission, which was promised according to St. Matthew.[9]

This commission conferred the power to rule in the Church. The historical record of the early years of the Church's activity demonstrates the fact that the Apostles acted in the capacity of rulers. St. Peter asserts his position as a leader and ruler in the Church at the Council of Jerusalem.[10] St. Paul in a discourse to the clergy at Ephesus, reminds them that they have been delegated to rule in the Church of God and that as bishops they are responsible for the souls committed to their charge.[11] In the Epistle to the Corinthians, St. Paul shows no timidity in making decisive statements concerning moral and religious practices. He assures the Christians at Corinth that he will set things in order when he makes his next visitation to the church at Corinth.[12] In the Epistle to Timothy, St. Paul gives some

[6] Smith, *o. c.*

[7] C. 752, 17; 5, 71, 8.

[8] *St. John*, XXI, 15.

[9] *St. Matthew*, XVI, 17-19.

[10] *Acts*, XV, 8.

[11] *Acts*, XX, 28.

[12] *I Cor.*, XI, 2, 33, 34.

direct regulations concerning the conduct of the members of the Ephesian congregation. He not only makes use of direct legislative power, but also delegates the enforcing of his regulations to the Bishop of Ephesus, St. Timothy.[13]

Unless the legislative power be supported and complemented by the judicial power, the former is of little avail. The executive without the judiciary is a weak and ineffective power. The laws are but written statements, intrinsically so many dead letters, and cannot enforce themselves. This is true of every society, it is true of an ecclesiastical society such as the Church. The wisdom of Christ foresaw and made provision for this need. He conferred on the Apostles the right to judge the actions of the members of the Church.[14] He empowered them to punish offenders and to exclude unrepentant offenders from the society of the Church.[15]

The Apostles made use of this power. The evidence of their conscious knowledge of it is found in their teachings and writings. St. Paul shows no hesitancy in denouncing the crime of incest reported to him from Corinth. The Apostle ordered the incestuous one to be excommunicated from the congregation lest his shameless conduct be a source of contamination to others.[16]

In another letter St. Paul instructs Timothy in the judicial process to be observed by a Bishop who officially receives an accusation against a cleric.[17]

The Councils. Other facts of history, which stand as evidence of the use of the judicial power in the Church, are the great Councils. An Ecumenical Council is an assemblage of the bishops of the world, who, in union with the Supreme Head of the Church, speak authoritatively on questions of doctrine and discipline. Arius and Arian heresy were condemned in the Council of Nice in the year 325. Nestorius and his heretical teachings

[13] *I Tim.*, V, 19.

[14] Wernz, *o. c.*, Tom. V, n. 80.

[15] *St. Matthew,* XVIII, 14-18.

[16] *I Cor.*, V, 3, 12, 13.

[17] *I Tim.*, V, 19.

were condemned in the year 431. The Council of Chalcedon was convened in the year 451 for the purpose of examining the strange teachings of Eutyches. Both he and his doctrines were condemned by the Council. The Council of Trent and the Council of the Vatican, famous for the great reforms which were accomplished in their sessions, are well known, being nearer the present period of history.

The Office of Judge in Justinian and Canon Law. The foregoing considerations establish the fact that the judiciary power has always been in evidence in the Church. The present dissertation is also concerned about the origin of the particular officer in whom this power is vested, that is the officialis mentioned in Canon 1573. It seems that his prototype can be traced to the pretor of Roman Law. The Catholic Church was the mistress of the world, the one secure organization in the times of the barbarian invasions. At this time, about the eleventh century, Roman Law was fast losing its force because of the disturbances in political affairs and also because of the legal system which the barbarians brought with them —the Jus Barbaricum. About this same time Canon Law began to be organized on a scientific basis, and codified. A concrete example of this is the Decretum of Gratian. The Church, the clergy adhered to the method and principles of Roman Law and Gratian uses legal terms when speaking of property, rights, etc., identical with those found in the Corpus Iuris Civilis of Justinian. There is also a great similarity in the titles and offices of legal personages.

To this may be added the opinion of Fournier.[18] This canonist holds that the position of the judge in the diocesan curia was firmly established in the diocesan curia in the first half of the twelfth century. His competency to hear cause within the jurisdiction of the bishop is affirmed by Pope Innocent IV in the constitution "Ro-

[18] Fournier, *o. c.*, p. 67.

mana ecclesia." It is the opinion of Fournier that the officialis of Canon Law is an institution which was first known in the Church in France. From there it spread to the other countries of the Continent but it was in France that the officialis acquired his complete development. In proof of this statement he cites the title "Officio Vicarii" of the Sextus of Boniface VIII.[19]

The Officialis in the Code. Canon 1573, § 1:

"Quilibet Episcopus tenetur officialem eligere cum potestate ordinaria iudicandi, a Vicario Generali distinctum, nisi parvitas diocesis aut paucitas negotiorum suadeat hoc officium ipsi Vicario Generali committi."

In this, the first paragraph of the Canon, the office of the diocesan judge "officialis" is established by the general law of the Church. By whom is he appointed? The officialis is appointed by the bishop of the diocese or the Ordinary of the locality. Under certain circumstances the appointment may be made by one not a consecrated bishop, e. g., the vicar capitular.[20] Both the abbot and the prelate nullius are privileged to appoint an official, since by Canon 215 they are to be understood as "ordinarius loci," ordinaries of a locality. This Canon must be read in the light of the foregoing Canon—1572. That Canon defines the judicial power of the "ordinarius loci" who may use this power in person or delegate it to others within his diocese or territory.

Is the bishop *bound* to appoint an official. The Canon uses the word "tenetur"—he is held to do so. The Code seems to anticipate the possibility of there being little need for the services of an official in certain localities. If such be the case in any diocese, then the bishop may appoint the vicar general to act in the capacity of judge also. The circumstances which justify this action on the part of the bishop are when the diocese is small, "par-

[19] Fournier, p. 70, 71; C. I. de off. v. I, 13 in VI.

[20] Can. 1573, § 7.

vitas,"[21] or the rare occurrence of judicial trials in the diocese, "paucitas negotiorum."[22] Hence it would seem to be the mind of the law that an official should be appointed in every diocese.

Noval makes the comment that it is wisely ordained that the judge in the diocese be a person other than the bishop. The bishop is the pastor of the diocese and there are so many duties which demand his time and attention that the settlement of disputes, etc., may well be left to the officialis. Moreover, the rendering of judgments in either contentious or criminal cases may be more difficult for the pastor and ruler of the diocese than for another who is but a member of the curia.[23]

The law specifies that the office of judge is to be distinct from that of the vicar general. It is the opinion of Pellegrini that before the promulgation of the Code the officialis and the vicar general were one and the same, at least the titles were used indiscriminately.[24]

Fournier is of the opinion that the present legislation which makes the two offices separate and distinct is but a return to an ancient regulation. It is his opinion that the condition in Italy which allowed the union of official and vicar general into one and the same appointment was the result of a special concession or legislation. He maintains that in France the distinction between these two officers in the curia was always recognized, both in appointments and in spheres of action.[25] Whatever the former discipline may have been, the present and future policy is governed by the Code. The officialis is an office in the diocesan curia is to be "a vicario generali distinctum."

Nature and Extent of the Power of the Officialis:

"Officialis unum constituit tribunal eum Episcopo loci; sed nequit iudicare causas quas Episcopus sibi reservat." [26]

[21] Can. 1573, § 1. [22] Can. 1573, § 1. [23] Noval, *o. c.*, 11-113.

[24] Pellegrini, Praxis Vicariorum P. 1, S. 1, subs., II, I.

[25] Fournier, *o. c.*, l. c. p. 8.

[26] Can. 1573, p. 2.

The tribunal or court of the official is to be considered as one and the same with that of the bishop, that is, of the same grade. This does not imply that the officialis is equal in person to the bishop. The officialis derives his jurisdiction from the bishop. The bishop has the power to limit the jurisdiction of the official by reservations of certain causes. But since the tribunal of the officialis is a court of the first instance, and since his jurisdiction extends to all persons and things within the diocese, it is said to be "unum tribunal cum Episcopo loci."

The bishop may limit the jurisdiction of the officialis by reserving or withholding certain causes from the jurisdiction of the court of the officialis. Noval thinks that these reservations are not to be so numerous as to change the character of the power of the officialis from that of ordinary to merely delegated power. Should it be necessary to apply to the bishop for faculties to judge in the majority of causes, causes reserved to the bishop, he would be acting as a delegated official rather than as one with continued and ordinary power.[27]

The Number of Officials in a Diocese:

"Officiali dari possunt adiutores, quibus nomen est vice-officialium." [28]

It follows logically from the term "officialis" in the first paragraph of this canon that there is to be but one such office in the curia. Should the need arise, because of the many cases coming in for hearing, the officialis is to be given assistants in the work. The paragraph quoted above justifies the appointment of these assistants and gives them the title of "vice-officials." They are appointed by the bishop, their work will be in the judiciary department of the diocese under the presidency of the official and D'Angelo is inclined to think that their power is ordinary, just as the power of the officialis.[29]

[27] Noval, *o. c.*, n. 114; D'Angelo, S. II, CI, p. 2.
[28] Can. 1573, p. 3.
[29] D'Angelo, *o. c.*, S. II, C. I, p. 3.

Noval writes that the vice-official "aequiparantur officiali in omnibus," as is clear from § 4 and § 5 (1573), and Canon 1577, § 2., C. 1578.

Qualifications. The Code requires that both the official and the vice-officials be priests.[30] Quoting Canon 626, Noval holds that they must be secular priests. The Canon cited reads as follows:

"Religiosus nequit . . . ad . . . officia promoveri, quae cum statu religioso componi non possint."

It has already been stated that a religious can not be appointed vicar general unless the diocese has been committed to the care of his religious community.[31] A religious may not act as procurator or advocate in tribunals outside of the religious community.[32] Neither may a religious fill the office of notary in the cause of the beatification of Saints.[33] Hence it is logical to argue that a religious may not be appointed official or vice-official. The reason for this prohibition is clearly stated in Canon 626, that is, lest the duties of such diocesan appointments interfere with the life and observance of the rule of the religious community.

Other requisites are that the names of the appointees be above reproach. It is also required that the official and vice-officials be doctors in Canon Law or at least conversant with the principles of the Code. The age requirement for these offices is thirty years.[34]

Removal. The official and likewise the vice-officials may be removed from office whenever the bishop deems their removal necessary. Paragraph five states, "sunt amovibiles ad nutum Episcopi." The bishop may recall these appointments for any reasonable cause. However, he is under no obligation to discuss the cause, much less

[30] Can. 1575, § 4.

[31] Can. 367.

[32] Can. 1657.

[33] Can. 2014.

[34] Can. 1573, § 4.

state his reasons to those whom he removes from the office.[35]

The official continues in office even though the episcopal see be vacated. He cannot be removed from office by the vicar capitular[36] except for a crime for which he has been convicted through judicial procedure.[37] When the newly appointed bishop takes charge of the see, the official must look to him for a confirmation of his position in the curia. It is not certain that this confirmation is necessary for the validity of the acts of the officialis for this condition is not stated in the Canon.

When the one person is both vicar general and official sede vacante the office of vicar general ceases ipso facto, the office of officialis does not cease.[38]

If the See be vacated and the officialis be chosen vicar capitular, he ceases to be officialis when he accepts the new dignity. Having accepted, he may then appoint a new officialis.[39]

Synodal and Prosynodal Judges.

Canon 1574. § 1. **In qualibet dioecesi presbyteri probatae vitae et in iure canonico periti, etsi extradioecesani, non plures quam duodecim eligantur ut potestate ab Episcopo delegata in litibus iudicandis partem habeant; quibus nomen esto iudicum synodalium aut prosynodalium si extra Synodum constituuntur.**

§ 2. **Quod ad eorum electionem, substitutionem, cessationem aut remotionem a munere attinet, serventur praescripta Canon 385-388.**

§ 3. **Nomine iudicum synodalium in iure veniunt quoque iudices prosynodales.**

History. It is the opinion of Canonists that the origin of these auxiliary judges, prosynodal judges, in the diocesan curia may be traced to an enactment of the Holy See in the latter part of the thirteenth century.[40] In certain causes it was necessary that the Holy See commis-

[35] Noval, *o. c.*, n. 116.
[36] Can. 1573, p. 6.; Can. 436.
[37] Noval, *o. c.*, n. 116.
[38] Can. 1573, p. 6.
[39] Can. 1573, p. 7.
[40] Noval, *o. c.*, n. 117.

sion ecclesiastical persons to execute a mandate, rescript, etc., because of the remote location of the party or cause concerned. Boniface VIII found it advisable to pass certain regulations lest unfit persons be appointed to carry out these important mandates and thus be the occasion of a particular church or person to suffer injustice as a result of unfitness or inefficiency of the judge. In the bull of Boniface VIII, "Statuimus," the Pontiff ordered:

"ut nullis nisi dignitate praeditis, aut personatum obtinentibus, seu ecclesiarum Cathedralium Canonicus, causae auctoritate litterarum Apostolicae Sedis, vel Legatorum eius de cetero non commitantur; nec audiantur alibi quam in civitatibus et locis insignibus ubi commode possit copia peritorum haberi." [41]

The main provisions in the foregoing quotation are that persons worthy and capable of negotiating affairs in the name of the Holy See be appointed. If the matter be judicial procedure, the cause must be heard in a place of some importance where the services of skilled jurists, "peritorum," may be had. It is evident that these provisions were motivated by a high regard for justice.

This consideration received the attention of the Fathers in the Council of Trent. In the twenty-fifth sessembled in Provincial Synods recall the statute of Pope Boniface VIII, "Statuimus" and appoint synodal sion " De Reformatione," it was decreed that bishops asjudges. ". . . statuit in singulis Conciliis Provincialibus, aut diocesanis aliquot personas, quae qualitates habeant, iuxta constitutionem Bonifatii VIII, quae incipit Statuimus: et alioquin ad id aptas designari, ut praeter Ordinarios locorum, iis etiam posthas, causae ecclesiasticae, ac spirituales, et ad forum ecclesiasticum pertinentes, in partibus relegandae commitantur. Et si aliquem illorum interim ex designatis mori contigerit, substituat ordinarius loci cum consilio capituli alium, etc." [42]

[41] Cap. 11, I, II, in VI.°

[42] Sess. XXV, *De ref.*, c. 10.

In substance this is the provision found in the Canon 1574 of the Code. As will be shown, the legislation of the Code on this point is more specific than former legislation in giving attention to method of appointment, the number, the qualifications and the field of action of these auxiliary judges in our present ecclesiastical judicial procedure. Today the chief function of the "synodal-judge," as the Code terms them, is to form a collegiate tribunal whose presiding judge may be either the bishop of the diocese or the officialis.[43]

In Canon 1574—already quoted, the general law for the Universal Church is stated relative to the office and person of the synodal judges. The office and function of a judge in ecclesiastical affairs has been stated in a previous chapter.[44]

Defined. A synodal judge is a priest selected by the Bishop at the time of the diocesan synod to act when so delegated at any future time in a judicial capacity. The diocesan synod referred to in this canon is that deliberative assembly held in the diocese in accord with the law of the Church, as stated in Canon 356. If a priest be called to this appointment at a time other than during the sessions of the diocesan synod, he is to be known, according to the Code, is a pro-synodal judge. The bishop may appoint as many as twelve, or fewer if he wishes.

Qualifications. The Code requires, that for this office in the curia, the candidate be a priest. He may be a priest from another diocese, and as in the offices in the diocesan curia previously considered, he is to be a secular priest. Quite naturally the law requires that he who is called to act in a legal capacity settling the contentions and strife of others be a man of high moral qualifications and blameless in his life. It is not necessary that he have attained a degree in Canon Law, but the synodal judge must have some knowledge of the contents of the

[43] Can. 1576; Noval, *o. c.*, n. 117.

[44] Cf. "Officialis," supra.

Code, if he is to act intelligently in matters of legal procedure.[45]

Election, Substitution, Removal of Synodal Judges. The process of election, substitution and removal from office of the synodal judges is governed by those prescriptions of the Code found in Canons 385, 386, 387, and 388.

Therein it is provided that synodal judges be appointed at the time of the diocesan synod. The names are proposed by the bishop for the approval of those assembled in council.[46] Vacancies occurring in the ranks of the judges, caused by death, removal or other circumstances may be supplied in the years intervening the convocation of synods. Judges appointed at times other than the regular synod are known as "pro-synodal" judges. In making such appointments the bishop is directed to take counsel with the Cathedral Chapter.[47] In this country the bishop will take counsel with the diocesan consultors. (Can. 423.)

Cessation of Office. The terms of tenure of office for synodal judges is a period of ten years. In the case of one appointed between synods, his office ceases with the convocation of the next diocesan synod.[48] The term of office for a substitute will be determined by the remaining term of the one whose vacancy he is filling.[49] The bishop, for any serious reason, may remove any one of these men from office. Before such action, however, he will present the matter for the consideration and counsel of the Cathedral Chapter,[50] or as stated before, of the diocesan consultors.

Paragraph three of Canon 1575 legislates that there is no distinction in authority or importance between a synodal and pro-synodal judge. Whenever the former term is used in the wording of a Canon, the latter is to be understood as well.

[45] Can. 1574, § 1.

[46] Can. 385.

[47] Can. 105, § 1.

[48] Can. 387, § 1.

[49] Can. 387, § 2.

[50] Can. 388.

Compared with Officialis. If one would compare the auxiliary or synodal judges which have just been considered with that of the Officialis and vice-officials it will be noted that they differ in manner of appointment, in the nature of the jurisdiction and stability of office. The officialis is appointed independently of the synod; the appointment of the synodal judge is approved by the synod. The jurisdiction of the officialis is ordinary, extending to all persons and causes coming within the competence of the Ordinary, excepting reservations; the jurisdiction of the synodal judge is delegated—for a particular time, place and cause. There is no time limit to the tenure of office of the officialis; the synodal judge loses his appointment at the end of ten years.

Field of Action for Synodal Judges. The Code seems to indicate the purpose and duties of the synodal judges in the phrase, "eligantur ut potestate ab Episcopo delegata in litibus iudicandis partem habeant."[51] The synodal judges are chosen, and in virtue of the jurisdiction which they receive from the bishop, they may assist in the settlement of disputes in the ecclesiastical courts. By some authors the synodal judge is called an auxiliary judge. This expresses the same idea.

The Code indicates another function to which the synodal judge may be called—that of assessor:

> **"Unicus iudex in quolibet iudicio duos assessores consulenten sibi adsciscere potest; quos tamen ex iudicibus synodalibus eligere debet."[52]**

Having considered the duty of synodal judge when acting as auxiliary, or associate judge, the latter duty of assessors will then be considered.

Collegiate Tribunals. A cause brought before an ecclesiastical court may be adjudged by one judge or by several judges. If the cause be presented in the courts

[51] Can. 1574, § 1; Noval, *o. c.*, n. 122; D'Angelo, *o. c.*, p. 25.
[52] Can. 1575.

where several judges are to render decision it is said to be tried before a collegiate tribunal. A collegiate tribunal may be composed of three, five or more judges. The legal procedure before such a tribunal will always proceed according to the vote of the majority and the vote of the majority will determine the decision or judgment of the court.

The collegiate tribunal is found in Roman procedure. According to Smith,[53] "The judges were chosen by lot out of those who were qualified to act. Both the plaintiff and the accused had the privilege of rejecting or challenging such judges as they did not like. The judges appointed according to the provisions of the Lex Licinia de Ambitu, B. C. 55, were called 'edititii'. . . . The judges voted by ballot and a majority determined the acquittal or condemnation of the accused. If the votes were equal, there was an acquittal. Each judge was provided with three tablets on one of which was marked A, Absolvo; on a second, C, Condemno; on a third, N. L., Non Liquet. The judges voted by placing one of these tablets in the urn, which was then examined for the purpose of ascertaining the votes. It was the duty of the magistrates to pronounce the sentence of the judges; in case of condemnation they were to adjudge the legal penalty; of acquittal, to declare the accused acquitted; and of doubt to declare that the matter must be further invesigated (amplius cognoscendum)."

Collegiate Tribunal Required by the Code. There are ecclesiastical causes in a diocese which demand judgment by several judges, or a collegiate tribunal. There are other ecclesiastical causes which may or may not be adjudged collegiately, according to the prudence of the bishop. Canon 1576, § 1, states:

"Reprobata contraria consuetudine et revocato quolibet contraria privilegio:

§ 1. Causae contentiosae de vinculo sacrae conditionis et

[53] Smith, *Dictionary of Greek and Roman Antiques*, "Iudex."

matrimonii, vel de iuribus aut bonis temporalibus cathedralis ecclesiae; itemque criminales in quibus res est de privatione beneficii inamovibilis aut de irroganda vel declarando excommunicatione, tribunali collegiali trium iudicum reservantur.

§ 2. Causae vero quibus agitur de delictis quae depositionis, privationis perpetuae habitus ecclesiastici, vel degradationis poenam important, reservantur tribunali quinque iudicum.

§ 3. Loci Ordinarius tribunali collegiali trium vel quinque iudicum cognitionem committere potest etiam aliarum causarum, idque praesertim quando de causis agitur quae, attentis temporis, loci et personarum adiunctis et materia iudicii, difficiliores et maioris momenti videantur."

This Canon emphasizes the necessity of the collegiate tribunal. Judgment rendered in a form other than that of a collegiate body of judges, a body composed of the number required by the Code for that particular cause would be invalid.[54]

Furthermore the above Canon specifies in what causes a collegiate tribunal is to be summoned. Some of the causes are contentious; others are criminal causes. A contentious cause is a cause arising out of a dispute between individuals. A criminal cause having as its object the punishment of a crime.[55]

The following causes are explicitly reserved to a tribunal of three judges:

a) Causes arising from a dispute as to the validity of the bond of Holy Orders or the validity of the matrimonial bond.

b) Causes arising from a dispute concerning the rights and the possessions of the Cathedral Church.

c) Criminal cases in which the point of issue is the privation of a permanent benefice ("inamovibilis"), or the removal or declaration of an excommunication. The sentence of excommunication here referred to is that which is the result of a judicial procedure, not the pun-

[54] "Reprobata contraria consuetudine . . . etc"—Can. 1576.

[55] Cicero, pro Caecina 2, quoted by Smith, *o. c.*, p. 648, 3.

ishment incurred lata sententia, or by very fact of the transgression of a particular law.[56]

A tribunal of five judges is required to hear the following causes:

a) Criminal causes, serious in their nature, meriting such punishment as deposition, or removal from office, as in the case of heretics, schismatics and clerical apostates according to the provisions of Canon 2314, § 1, n. 2.

b) Similarly a crime of so grave a nature as to be punished by permanent divestiture of the religious habit, or the more severe penalty of degradation or a reduction from the clerical to the lay state in life, according to the prescriptions of Canon 2379, must be tried by a collegiate tribunal of five judges.

c) In the third paragraph of Canon 1576, the Code permits the bishop to entrust causes other than the above to a collegiate tribunal composed of three or five judges. When all circumstances are considered, such as the time, the place and persons in litigation, seem to indicate the need of great caution and prudence on the part of the one rendering the decision, then the safer method of a judgment rendered by the collegiate body of judges should be followed.[57]

The Code leaves the matter of choosing the judges entirely to the prudence and wisdom of the Ordinary. He may select them from the number of diocesan synodal judges. He need not be influenced by circumstances of seniority, but may select and delegate as prudence dictates for a particular cause.[58]

The Assessors.

The assessors are mentioned in Canon 1575. An assessor is a specialist who is associated with a judge. By his expert advice and counsel he assists the judge in the consideration of intricate and perplexing questions

[56] Can. 2225.

[57] Can. 1576, § 3.

[58] Can. 1576, § 3.

connected with a legal cause. The assessor has no official voice in the decision of the cause.

In the old law, before the Code, the practice of calling in the assessors was left to the conscience of the judge. Should the judge call in an assessor and there were no particular need for such services, the judge personally was bound to recompense the assessor.[59]

The Code prescribes that to every judge is allowed the services of two assessors. The cost of their services is to be borne not by the judge but by the litigants in the case. The synodal judges may also act in this capacity, is selected by the bishop, according to the provisions of Canon 1575.

Controversies Involving Religious. Who is to be the judge in causes in which the rights and property of religious are the issue? If the litigants in the cause be men of the same religious order, the cause will be judged by the religious superior. Generally this religious superior will be either the Provincial Superior of the Order or the local Abbot of the monastery according to the nature of the case.[60]

Should a dispute arise between two provinces of a religious community, the cause must be brought before the Supreme Moderator of that particular community, unless the constitutions of the community have other provisions.[61]

The Ordinary of the place is judge *in prima instantia,* or in the initial hearing of the proceedings in the following causes: Disputes between—

a) Religious who are members of the same community, it being non-exempt or a lay community.

b) Religious (moral or physical persons) of different communities.

c) A religious in litigation with a secular priest.

d) Religious and laity.[62]

[59] Verm.-Creusen, *o. c.*, vol. 3, n. 37.

[60] Can. 1579, § 1.

[61] Can. 1579, § 2.

[62] Can. 1579, § 3.

The Code offers a suggestion to the bishops concerning the handling of controversies and prosecuting crime which may be given here. In effect, the Code advises that although the bishop may always preside over the tribunals in the diocese, either as an individual judge, or as the presiding judge in a collegiate tribunal, nevertheless, it is prudent that criminal causes and contentious causes be left to the ordinary tribunal. By the ordinary tribunal is meant to the officialis or the synodal judges of his curia.[63]

Causes in Ecclesiastical Tribunals.

Ecclesiastical Causes. Having reviewed the question of judges and tribunals according to the Canons of the Code of Canon Law it is well to give a brief statement of what is to be understood by a legal cause in the diocesan tribunal. There are two divisions of these causes, *contentious* and *criminal.* The first, *contentious,* is a dispute or contention as to the possession or retention of rights, goods, or property. It is to be understood of course, that the Church in the Code is legislating solely for those, who by Baptism, are members of the Church, (Can. 87). Hence the contentious cause which finds its way before the bishop or the officialis or the collegiate tribunal of the diocesan court, must be a matter within the jurisdiction of the ecclesiastical court. Thus it may be the question of a disputed boundary between two parishes, the question about the removal or appointment to a benefice, a disputed debt between pastor and parishioners.

The prosecution of an ecclesiastical offence is a *criminal cause.* The Code outlines for us the elements which constitute an ecclesiastical delictum. By a delictum in ecclesiastical law there is to be understood an external and morally imputable violation of a law to which is appended an ecclesiastical sanction, a sanction which is at least indeterminate. A delictum, therefore,

[63] Can. 1578.

is a species of sin, the result of an external act which may be morally imputed to the one who performed it. An internal act of the intellect cannot be an ecclesiastical delictum. The Code affords many examples of ecclesiastical delicta or those actions which come within the competence of the ecclesiastical courts and for which the responsible party may be prosecuted and punished according to principles of ecclesiastical penology.

In the third part of the second section of Book Five we find the Canons which deal with penalties for certain specified crimes: the following are mentioned—

a) Crimes against the faith and unity of the Church, such as apostasy, heresy, schism, those who spread false doctrines or are actively associated with heretics in their divine service.

b) Crimes against religion, such as profanation of the consecrated species, sins of blasphemy, perjury, etc.

c) Crimes against ecclesiastical authorities, persons or possessions. This includes such crimes as frauds, deceptions in the elections of the Sovereign Pontiff, legislators who interfere with the liberty and rights of the Church, those who join the masonic society, etc.

For the above mentioned and many similar offences the Church rightfully claims it within her jurisdiction to prosecute and punish those who are found guilty. Her purpose is to accomplish the salvation of the delinquent, if possible, as well as to safeguard her life as a true society.

Auditors and Relators.

In the judiciary department of the curia there are officers other than the judge, whose duty it is to assist in the work entailed in the conduct of a judicial process. Of these officers, the first to come to our consideration are the auditors and the relators.[64]

Auditors. An auditor is a cleric, who, by reason of jurisdiction delegated to him, is empowered to cite wit-

[64] Art. II, Cap. I, Tit. II, Sec. I, Book IV, C. I. C.

nesses before an ecclesiastical court, hear their testimony and perform other judicial acts, in keeping and within the limits of the commission through which he acts.[65] Wernz, considering the auditor in a more limited sense, states that the auditor is one, who, in ancient practise, was commissioned by the Holy See to study up the particulars of an entire case, or some particular points of a case. The result of this research was then presented to the judge in the proceedings, and he rendered the sentence.[66] The auditor is also known in legal terminology as the instructor, or the " iudex Instructor." [67]

History. The office of auditor is found in the Roman Curia even in the Middle Ages. They were commissioned by the Holy See to hear certain ecclesiastical causes. The place where these cases were heard was called the auditorium.[68] The most important auditors in the Roman Curia were the Auditors of the Roman Rota. To this famous body or college of auditors the Roman Pontiffs turned for legal advice and help by sending certain causes to them for their earnest consideration.[69] According to Durantis this body of auditors was constituted as a collegium about the thirteenth century. At that time they gave their time to the study of legal causes and counseled the principal judge in legal causes or certain points of law but rendered no decisions themselves.[70] In the course of time this body of auditors received jurisdiction from the Roman Pontiff and thus qualified to render decisions in contentious causes.[71]

As a result of more recent legislation the auditors, or cognitores, as they are termed in the Decretals, have become a part of the bishop's curia. The Instruction of

[65] Vermeersch, *o. c.*, n. 40.

[66] Wernz, VI, n. 137; Cap. 10, X, de fide instr. II, 22.

[67] Vermeersch, vol. III, n. 40.

[68] Dig., 1, 22, 5.

[69] Wernz, *o. c.*, vol. VI, n. 138.

[70] Wernz, quoting Durantis, *o. c.*, vol. VI, p. 124.

[71] Greg. XVI, *Regal. Giud.*, page 327.

the Sacred Congregation of Bishops and Regulars,[72] gave certain regulations concerning auditors. In the instruction the auditors are referred to as the "actorum Instructor," and in article 29 as the "causae instructor." This latter expression is found in the Code. Canons 1580 which is the first in the article devoted to the auditor uses this phrase, "auditores, seu actorum instructores."[73]

Auditors in the Code. The first point which is quite clear from Canon 1580 is that the appointment of auditors in the curia of the diocese is left to the discretion of the bishop.[74] He may choose one or many, according to the requirements for the causes in the diocese, and the bishop will determine whether the appointment is to be permanent or for a particular judicial process. If the bishop does not make the appointment, the office is to be filled by an appointee of the judge.

Eligible for the Office. Can the bishop select a layman and appoint him to act as auditor or instructor in a cause? D'Angelo answers this question in the affirmative, provided that the layman be merely an instructor in the process, that is a legal advisor or counsellor. If, however, the instructor is to be appointed with true jurisdiction in the cause, if he is to have a voice in the decision, then the one appointed must be a cleric.[75]

The auditors in the diocesan tribunal may be selected from the number of synodal judges.[76] The auditors in a tribunal of a religious community will always be selected from among the members of the community in which the litigation arises.[77] In this matter due regard must be shown for the constitution and rules of the community.

[72] Inst. S. C. EE. at RR., June 11, 1880, art. 12 and art. 29.
[73] Can. 1580, § 1.
[74] § 1.
[75] D'Angelo, *o. c.*, p. 72; Noval, *o. c.*, n. 133; Can. 193.
[76] Can. 1581.
[77] Can. 1581.

Duties of the Auditor. The duties of the auditor must be clearly stated in the mandate or the appointment which comes from the bishop. Generally the auditor will be expected to perform the following duties:

1. The auditor will summon the witnesses to appear before the tribunal.

2. He will examine the witnesses and hear their testimony.

3. He will be prepared to give advice and information in the judicial procedure, in accordance with the directions of the bishop who appoints him.

The foregoing enumeration of the duties of the auditor is merely demonstrative, that is, the duties which are usually committed to the auditor. His capacity in each case will be determined by the wording of the document of his appointment.[78] The possible extent of the activity of the auditor is discussed by Noval as follows:

(1) The auditors may be commissioned to take care of the many duties detailed in a judicial proceeding from the "contestatio litis" usque "ad publicationem processus."

(2) In contentious cases the auditor may be ordered to make the necessary preparations for the "introductio causae," or the formal opening of the cause. These preparatory duties include, the acceptance or the rejection of the libellus or the allegation in which the charge is made by the plaintiff; the sending out of the first summons to the parties in dispute and also the "contestatio litis" or formal opening of the cause before a court. In all criminal causes and causes arising from some notorious crime, the summons sent to the criminals in the cause must be sent by the Ordinary.[79]

(3) The auditor may not be commissioned to perform those acts in the process through which the cause is defined or settled, in either contentious or criminal causes. This excludes his officiating at the following:

[78] Noval, *o. c.*, n. 135.

[79] Can. 1964, § 3.

a) *Iusiurandum decisorium,* that is, the settlement of the dispute, or the point in dispute, by means of a statement of the proper party in the suit, made under oath and with the approval of the judge.[80]

b) *Transactio,* the effect of which is known in the Code as a *compositio* or *concordia,* is the settlement of a contentious cause by an agreement between the parties. This of course was negotiated in the presence of a court official other than the judge.[81]

c) *Correptio judicialis,* which is one of the means for the correction of delinquents suggested in ecclesiastical penal law.[82] This remedy may be made use of in certain circumstances in place of a punishment. In the case of a *recidivus,* repeated admonitions may increase the final guilt.[83]

(4) In an appeal, "appelatio," the auditor may be designated to take charge of a particular point pertaining to the new proofs to be established, or the strengthening of proofs offered in the first instance of the trial. Thus he may recall and hear the testimony of a witness who was unjustly excluded from the first hearing.[84]

(5) The auditor is forbidden by the Code to conclude any cause by a definitive or final sentence. This act lies within the jurisdiction of the judge who presides over the court.[85]

The Removal of an Auditor from Office. The auditor may be removed from his office by the one who appointed him, hence by the Ordinary, or the judge. He may be removed at any moment of the process, either before or after the *contestatio litis.* The Code adds, "iusta tamen de causa," that is, the removal must be for a just cause and should be accomplished without prejudice or injury to those parties who are the principals in the suit.[86]

[80] Can. 1834; Can. 1836, n. 3.

[81] Can. 1925; Can. 1928.

[82] Can. 2306.

[83] Can. 2309.

[84] Noval, *o. c.*, n. 136.

[85] Can. 1582.

[86] Can. 1583.

The Relator in a Collegiate Tribunal. The relator, according to the Code, is one of the judges of a collegiate tribunal who is selected by the presiding judge as the one who is to render a written statement of the proceedings within the judicial assembly. This statement is to be a record of the evidence, allegations, proofs, judicial opinions and all important pronouncements of the judges which may influence the final sentence.[87]

Origin. Noval agrees with Schmalzgruber, whom he quotes, in the statement that this office was especially needed and used in the major tribunals of civil rulers. According to Noval, it is an established legal custom to appoint a relator in collegiate tribunals in the civil courts in Spain.[88]

In ecclesiastical procedure, the relator is found in the ancient pontifical tribunal of the Roman Rota. This being one of the highest courts in ecclesiastical procedure, and was composed as it is today of several auditors. To this judicial body the Pope referred disputed questions for study and counsel.[89] By the present legislation of the Code, the relator now finds his place, according to the general law, in the judiciary of the bishop's curia.

Canon Referring to Relator. Can. 1584:

"Tribunalis collegialis praeses debet unum de judicibus collegii ponentem seu relatorem designare qui in coetu iudicum de causa referat et sententias in scriptis redigat; et ipsi idem praeses potest alium ex iusta causa substituere."

There are three important points concerning the relator determined by the above quoted Canon. He is to be appointed by the senior or presiding judge of the tribunal. The duty to make the appointment is not imposed absolutely; the Code uses the word "debet." The services of the relator are most necessary and helpful. On this point Noval writes: "quia magnopere expedit ut

[87] Can. 1584; Vermeersch-Creusen, vol. III, n. 40.

[88] Noval, *o. c.*, n. 132.

[89] Lega, *o. c.*, vol. II, n. 66.

iam inde ab introductione uniuscujusque causae adsit unus qui examini ipsius specialiter incumbat, progressus, vicissitudines, et praecipuas probationes adnotet, conclusiones inde emergentes colligat, quas deinceps opportune proponat aliis iudicibus pro eorundum illustratione, cum moraliter impossible sit quod quilibet iudex tribunalis collegialis pari conatu examini singularum causarum vacet." The purpose, as stated by Noval, is for the convenience of the judges of the cause, that an official record of the case may be had for their instruction as an aid to a just and intelligent discussion of the cause as presented in the trial.[90]

The one to be appointed must be, according to this Canon, one from the collegiate tribunal on which he is to serve. Noval is of the opinion that the praeses may not appoint himself to act as relator. His reasons for this opinion are based on the context of the law, and also because of the duties incumbent upon him as presiding judge, such as the instruction of the cause and more detailed duties if it be a court of second instance.

Method of Appointing—Removal. The appointment may be made orally, a document is not necessary.[91] The duration of the appointment depends upon the judge who makes the selection. The removal may be made at any time for any cause which seems just to the praeses.

Juridical Competence:

"Iudex antequam aliquem ad suum trahat tribunal et iudicaturus sedeat, videat utrum ipse sit competens, necne."

In this paragraph of Canon 1609, the Code imposes the obligation upon the judge, to be certain as to his competence to adjudge the persons and the causes which are brought to his tribunal. What is meant by competence in a judge? When is a tribunal competent?

Competence, in the legal sense, means the qualification or the capability in a judge, by reason of which, he may

[90] Noval, *o. c.*, n. 137.

[91] Noval, *o. c.*, 139.

render a decision in the disputes and crimes submitted to his court. Competence implies, and in fact is, jurisdiction. Competence is jurisdiction limited and specified. The limitation may be a limitation as to certain persons who come within the scope of a particular judge's powers. The limitation may also be in regard to certain causes which may be legally submitted to a court.

From this it follows that a judge has not universal power. The official in the diocesan curia has well determined limits. These limits he may not exceed. An example of certain *persons* who are exempted from the court of the diocesan official are given in Canon 1557:

§ 1. Ipsius Romani Pontificis dumtaxat ius est iudicandi:

§ 1. Eos qui supremum tenent populorum principatum horumque filios ac filias eosve quibus ius est proxime succedendi in principatum;

§ 2. Patres Cardinales;

§ 3. Legatos Sedis Apostolicae, et in criminalibus Episcopos, etiam titulares . . . etc.

Certain *causes* are also withheld from the court of a diocesan official:

§ 3. Alias causas quas Romanus Pontifex ad suum advocaverit iudicium, videt iudex quem ipsemet Romanus Pontifex designaverit.[92]

From this quotation it is evident that the Holy See can summon to itself or to specially appointed judges the causes which are deemed worthy of particular consideration. The bishop too can reserve causes to himself, thereby limiting the competence of the official in the curia in such matters:

Officialis unum tribunal constituit cum episcopo loci: sed nequit iudicare causas quas episcopus sibi reservat.[93]

In accordance with this regulation of the Code, the officialis has no jurisdiction over the causes which the bishop of the diocese reserves to himself for decision.

[92] Can. 1557, § 3; 1609.

[93] Can. 1573, § 3.

Reason for Limitations. Why does the positive law assign limits to the power of jurisdiction of judges, thus determining their competency? Since the limitation is accomplished through reservations, the reason or foundation may lie in the *purpose* of reservations in the internal forum.

The limitation of jurisdiction is called "reservatio" in the Code. By this process, those who by ordinary right have the power of hearing confessions and inflicting censures can also summon certain causes to themselves for judgment, by limiting the power of granting absolution in their inferiors:

Qui ordinario iure possunt audiendi confessiones potestatem concedere aut fere censuras, possunt quoque, . . . nonnullos casus ad suum avocare iudicium, inferioribus absolvendi potestatem limitantes.[94]

Although the Code does not state the *reason* for this summoning to a higher court, it may be assumed that the reservation is founded in disciplinary rather than penal reasons. It is not intended as a punishment for the delinquent, but rather a regulation through which the crime will be given the expert attention of a higher court. The reasons adduced in favor of this opinion are as follows:

(1) A reservation "per se" is not listed among the canonical penalties.[95]

(2) The limitation of jurisdiction affects the confessor directly by limiting his power to grant absolution. The penitent is affected indirectly in so far as only certain confessors can absolve from the sin. In civil judgments the more serious crimes must be tried in higher courts, in order to safeguard the proper exercise of judicial procedure.[96]

(3) An Instruction from the Holy Office, July 13th, 1916, advises Ordinaries to "strive to form throughout their dioceses, learned, pious and prudent confessors and

[94] Can. 893; § 1.

[95] Can. 2255.

[96] Dargin—"Reserved Cases," p. 11.

to these they should suggest those remedies which are adapted to check growing vices and which they themselves would use if the penitent were sent to them." [97] It is remedies suggested in the above Instruction, not penalties.

If the point developed through the foregoing paragraphs may apply equally to reservation in the external forum whereby the jurisdiction of a judge is limited, it may be safely stated in answer to our question that the purpose of reservations in the external forum is likewise disciplinary. Therefore, for more expert juridical treatment, some causes, specified both in general and particular law, are summoned to a higher court.

Incompetence in Judges. An official who does not possess the necessary jurisdiction is said to be incompetent. Incompetence is *relative* or *absolute*. If the incompetence be *absolute,* the sentence of the judge is invalid.[98] Thus the Roman Pontiff alone is competent to judge the ecclesiastical causes of civil rulers, the sons and daughters of these rulers, the Cardinals, etc.[99] If the incompetence be *relative,* the judge being unable to claim jurisdiction by reason of the titles enumerated in the Code, Can. 1560-Can. 1568, the sentence is valid but illicit.[100] Thus the Code regulates that the forum for an "actio de spolio" is the court of the Ordinary where the thing (over which the litigation arose) is located. Should it happen that the trial is brought before the official of the neighboring diocese, he would be relatively incompetent—presupposing that in this case the latter official had no claim to the case by the title of preoccupancy or other just title.

It is most important then, that the judge make sure that he has the proper jurisdiction, that he is competent to hear the cause before he attempts to carry through the judicial procedure.[101]

[97] *A. A. S.*, vol. VIII, p. 313.

[98] Can. 1558.

[99] Can. 1557.

[100] Can. 1559.

[101] Noval, *o. c.*, n. 191.

Forum. The word *forum* occurs frequently in treatises on the ecclesiastical judge and ecclesiastical procedure. Reference is made to the internal and the external forum, the ecclesiastical and the civil forum, the diocesan forum, the matrimonial forum and other similar modifications of this term.

In ancient Rome, the forum was the place of public assembly. Public disputes and discussions as well as legal procedure found place for expression in the forum. In later years, the forum became the place of legislative assemblages and finally came to be the place known as the tribunal of justice.

In ecclesiastical law the word forum may be used to designate the person of the judge, the court or locality, where justice is administered and again to signify the judicial power, that is the power of judging in disputes and crimes.

The following division may be given to indicate the important modifications of the forum in a discussion on ecclesiastical procedure:

(1) A *competent* forum is a forum with full capacity to adjudge the cause brought before it. An *incompetent* forum is one lacking the legal capacity to adjudge a cause, having no jurisdiction over the person or the cause.

(2) The *internal* forum (forum conscientiae or forum poli), is that jurisdiction by which the Church deals with questions concerning the welfare of individual Christians and their relations to God. The *external* forum has reference to matters touching the public and social good of the corporate body. The absolution from sin is proper to the internal forum. The concession of faculties or the power to absolve, belongs to the activity of the external forum.

(3) The *constitutional* forum is that forum which is constituted by the law, and constituted exclusively by the law for the particular cause which it hears. Canon 1557, § 1, n. 1, n. 2, n. 3, furnishes an example of this. The *prorogued forum* (forum prorogationis) is also consti-

tuted by law, but by the law a choice of fora is permitted and the one determined by the choice of the parties is the prorogued forum. This is exemplified in Canon 1566, § 2.

(4) The *common* or *general* forum is that tribunal which is constituted for all persons and all causes, for example the diocesan forum.[102] The *singular* or *special* forum is constituted for special persons or causes. The causes of exempt religious have a special forum.[103] The tribunal of the Holy Office is to be sought when the cause is one concerning the doctrines of Faith.

(5) A forum is *universal* if its power extends to the Universal Church; otherwise it is a *particular* forum.

(6) A forum is *ordinary* when by a general law persons or causes are declared subject to it; a person or cause referred to a forum by way of exception, constitutes an *extraordinary* forum.

(7) The forum *necessarium,* or *necessary* forum is the forum which is prescribed by Law.[104] The *voluntary* forum is the forum selected by the parties, the choice being permitted by law.[105]

(8) The forum *absolutum* (*absolute competens*), is that forum which is established by law as *the forum,* absolutely excluding an approach to another tribunal under pain of rendering both the judicial process and the sentences null.[106] If two courts be equally competent to hear a cause, the fora are then *relatively* (*relative*) competent.[107]

Determining the Competent Form. Since it is most important that a cause be tried in the court of a judge having proper jurisdiction for the cause, the following points must be noted in determining the competence of the judge, or of the forum. It has been shown that the basis of limiting the competence is merely direct result of certain reservations, by which certain causes and certain persons are summoned to another, at times to a

[102] Can. 1573.

[103] Can. 1579, § 1.

[104] Can. 1560.

[105] Can. 1561.

[106] Can. 1576, § 1; Can. 1557.

[107] Can. 1560.

higher court. What are the criteria according to which these distinctions are made? Does limited competence always imply that the judge is absolutely incompetent to hear a cause reserved to another judge?

Roberti answers these questions by showing a limitation of competence does not effect absolute incapacity in every case. The limitations may be relative, "prorogabilis" or absolute, "improrogabilis." If under stated conditions the law permits an extension of the competence of the court, the parties in the suit consenting, the competence is relative. If the law admits of no extension of the competence of the court, the limitation is absolute and the strict specifications of the law must be observed as to the hearing of causes under pain of nullity.

An example of relative competence is found in Can. 1565:

"Ratione contractus pars conveniri potest coram ordinario loci in quo contractus initus est vel adimpleri debet."

This means that a contract drawn up in the diocese "X," and the fulfillment of the contract is to take place in the diocese "Y," the judge in either diocese is competent, should the cause come to the courts. The choice of the judges made by the plaintiff in taking the cause to court determines the competence.

On the contrary if the law prohibits any extension of competence, declaring that a judge, in a particular tribunal, and he alone may try a cause, to the exclusion of all other judges and tribunals, the competence of such a court is "absolute improrogabilis." Canon 1567 illustrates this principle:

§ 1. **Ipsius Romani Pontificis dumtaxat ius est iudicandi:**

1.° **Eos qui supremum tenent populorum principatum horumque filios ac filias eosve quibus ius est proxime suscedendi in principatum.**

2.° **Patres Cardinales, etc.**

From this quotation of the Code it is established that the Roman Pontiff, and he alone, is competent to hear the causes of civil rulers, also the legal procedure involving their sons, daughters and their immediate successors in line of office. The Cardinals and all others enumerated in this Canon are to be tried by the Roman Pontiff.

In answer to the question concerning the criteria or norms which govern limitation, of jurisdiction, they may be narrowed down to four main distinctions. The limitations are made with respect to:

(1) Persons—that is, "ex subiecto."

(2) The nature of the cause—"ex obiecto."

(3) The rank or grade of the tribunal—whether it be a court of first or second instance.

(4) The territorial limits—affecting either the judge or the plaintiff in the cause.

Absolute Competence. Criteria based on either *subjective* or *objective* considerations, that is to say, if the limitation concerns specified persons or specified causes, the *competence is absolute* in that judge designated by the law. Hence the law: "Romanus Pontifex a nemine judicari potest." [108] The Pope is above all jurisdiction, hence cannot submit to the jurisdiction of any judge.[109] The Cardinals and other persons and causes enumerated in Canon 1557 may be tried only by that tribunal specified in the law. All other tribunals are absolutely incompetent.

The limitation regulating the process of a trial should there be an appeal from a lower to a higher court, likewise renders the higher court incompetent to hear the cause except on the same "causa petendi" as introduced in the first instance. This competence, or incompetence is absolute.[110]

Relative Competence. Competence which is determined by territorial limits, admits of the extension of competence and is relative competence.[111] The forum delicti,[112] and the forum of domicile or quasi-domicile,[113] likewise the forum of the traveller in Rome [114] and many others mentioned in the Code are illustrations of relative competence.

[108] Can. 1556.

[109] Can. 1556.

[110] Can. 1571.

[111] Can. 1561.

[112] Can. 1566.

[113] Can. 1561.

[114] Can. 1562, § 1.

THE COMPETENT FORUM
(Can. 1556—Can. 1568.)

- I. *Absolute Competence* (none other can try cause.) C. 1557.
  - For Rom, Pontiff personally.
    1. Princes (Kings), Supreme Rulers, and Immediate Successors and wives and children.
    2. Cardinals—all even " in petto."
    3. Legates, Nuncios, Apostolic Delegates.
    4. All bishops in criminal causes.
  - Roman Tribunals. (Rota and Segnatura.)
    1. Bishops in Residence in contentious cases, with exception of fiscal cases.
    2. Dioceses and other moral persons having no Superior beneath the Supreme Pontiff, e. g. exempt religious orders, monastic congregations, etc.
- Relative Competence C. 1559—c. 1568
  - General Prin. C. 1559.
    1. In first instance defendant *must* appear before one of the following tribunals—otherwise trial is illicit.
    2. Other judges are *relative* incompetent and must refuse cause and defendant can place exceptio.
    3. Actio sequitur forum rei.
  - *Forum Necessarium.* no option determined in law— (C. 1560.)
    1. *de spolio* before Ord. rei sitae.
    2. *beneficium*—Ord. of place of ben.
    3. *administration*—ubi geritur administratio.
    4. *inheritance*—domicile of testator.
  - *Forum Liberum* " potest " C. 1561—C. 1568
    1. *rat. dom.*—coram Ord. loci dom.
       - a) *peregrinus* is " at home " in Urbe may choose proper Ord.
       - b) *peregrinus* in Urbe for one year may refuse proper Ord.
       - c) *vagus*—loco commorationis.
       - d) *religiosus*—loco domus suae.
    2. *rat. rei sitae*—loco rei sitae for actio in rem.
    3. *rat. contractus*—in loco contractus initi vel adimplendi.
    4. *rat. delicti*—in loco patrato deli.
    5. *rat. connexionis causarum* all connected to be tried by same judge.

CHAPTER IV.

The Promotor of Justice—The Defender of the Bond.

Can. 1586: **"Constituatur in diocesi promotor iustitiae et defensor vinculi: ille pro causis tum contentiosis in quibus bonum publicum, Ordinarii iudicio, in discrimen vocari potest, tum criminalibus; iste pro causis in quibus agitur de vinculo sacrae ordinationis aut matrimonii."**

This canon prescribes that the offices of promotor of justice and the defender of the bond—"public defender," should be established in every diocese. The former may be summoned by the ordinary to appear in either contentious or criminal causes of sufficient importance to demand this special attention. The latter is the official defender of the bond whenever there may be a dispute as to the validity of Sacred Orders or the existence of a valid matrimonial contract.

Promotor of Justice. This promotor or procurator in ecclesiastical procedure is to be appointed by the legitimate ecclesiastical authority. In the diocesan curia the appointment will come from the ordinary. The duties of this ecclesiastical officer will be the defense of the rights of the Church, through judicial procedure, in contentious and criminal causes. The promotor of justice may appear either as plaintiff or defendant.[1]

His duties consist in the safeguarding of ecclesiastical law and the prosecution of crime. Personal knowledge of an ecclesiastical crime will mean that he must take legal action against it. Should notification of a crime be brought to him, he must investigate the information, act as the guardian of the law, and at once begin proceedings with a view of punishing the delinquents. The position of the promotor of justice in ecclesiastical law, may

[1] Bouix, *o. c.*, I, p. 472, and Instr. S. C. Ep. and Reg. June, 1880, *A. A. S.*, vol. VI.

be likened to the position of the state-attorney in the governmental system of this country.

History. How far back in history can one go in tracing the origin of the promotor of justice? In their studies of the question canonists have gone back to the Corpus Iuris Civilis of Roman Law. In the Digest, for example, such titles as, "de procuratoribus et defensoribus,[2] and in another place, "de officio procuratoris Caesaris,[3] are found. Similar titles are to be found in the Code of the Corpus.[4] Noval suggests that even though the name "procurator" is found in these ancient sources, yet it is merely the name and not the same as the modern institution of ecclesiastical law.[5]

Wernz answers the question as to the origin of the promotor of justice by stating that this ecclesiastical office is based on a notion of a similar office in the civil courts of France. This was the office of the "ministere public," the director of public prosecutions. In the old French law, this minister was also known as the "procureurs du roi"—of the XIII century.

Cardinal Lega does not agree with this opinion. In the opinion of this great canonist, the fiscal procurator had his beginning or origin in Canon Law. He writes: "Historia Procuratoris Fiscalis tenebris obvolvitur remotioris antiquitatis ut certe in iure canonico suum initium habet."[6] This beginning, according to Cardinal Lega, dates from the appointment of the Grand Inquisitor by the Pope.[7] This Inquisitor appointed by Pope Innocent III was a special but permanent judge. He acted in the name of the Pope and in virtue of a direct delegation from the Holy See. It was the duty of the Inquisitor to deal legally with crimes against the Faith.

[2] D. III., 3.

[3] D. 1, 19.

[4] C. XI, 72, de procuratoribus.

[5] Noval, De Processibus, n. 140.—"iniure romanorum nomen erat sed institutum non erat."

[6] Lega, *De Judiciis Eccl.*, vol. I, pag. 171.

[7] Lega, *o. c.*, page 173.

He was to act at all times according to the established rules of canonical procedure and could fix only the customary penalties prescribed by Canon Law.[8]

Even before the decrees of the Fourth Lateran Council, by which the judicial office of Inquisitor was strictly and formally established, Lega points out that the Bishops of the Church were ever the public authority in the Church, ready to take legal action against crime and vice. In the course of time the bishops delegated this power to the "testes synodales." The duty of these synodal officers was to guard the observance of law and make the necessary inquisition into ecclesiastical crimes. The "testes synodales" were later replaced by the "fiscales episcoporum" also known as the "vicarii foranei" or the rural deans.[9]

In France and Spain. The bishops of France had made use of this type of officer in their curia even before the pontificate of Pope Benedict XIV. In the sixteenth century the bishops of France appointed curial officers whose duty it was to promote or direct the investigation of ecclesiastical crime—"promoventes inquisitiones." Noval quotes a document of the Sacred Congregation of the Consistory, "Hispalensis," Sept., 1559 in which mention is made of a "promotor," thus showing the knowledge and approval of this ecclesiastical office in the Church in Spain in the sixteenth century.

In Italy. The office of fiscal procurator was instituted for the diocese and province of Rome by Pope Benedict XIII. The letter through which the institution was made was issued June 12, 1724. Italy adopted the office later than France.

A document issued by the Sacred Congregation of Bishops and Regulars, Instruction of June, 1880, directed that the office of promotor be established in every diocesan curia throughout the world. Hence Canon 1586 of

[8] Cath. Ency., art. *Inquisition.*

[9] Benedict XIV, *De Synodo Dioc.* c. 3, n. 8.

the Code is substantially a repetition of this Instruction of the Sacred Congregation of Bishops and Regulars. The promotor of justice, by general law, is now declared to be a very necessary officer in every diocese. This officer is appointed in exempt clerical religious communities and is to preside over the tribunals in accordance with the specifications of the Code.[10]

Defender of the Bond. The defender of the bond is an ecclesiastical officer whose duty it is to stand firmly for the truth and strict justice when there is a dispute concerning the validity of a marriage or the validity of Sacred Orders. As Noval writes, the defender of the bond is but a species of the office of the promotor of justice. His supervision in the present capacity is over the marriage tie or the bond of Sacred Orders.[11]

History. This particular office in matrimonial trials was instituted by Pope Benedict XIV in the constitution, "Dei miseratione," Nov. 3, 1741. It is mentioned and confirmed in the later constitution "Nimiam licentiam," of March 1743, issued by the same Pontiff. This most wisely conceived ecclesiastical institution was retained by many later Instructions from the Sacred Congregations, for example in the Instruction of the S. C. de Prop. Fide ad Stat. Foed. Am. of Sept. 1883. The title and office is retained in the Code as shown in the Canon quoted at the opening of this chapter.

Purpose. The purpose in instituting this office was to provide an official person whose sole duty would be to stand for, and legally defend the matrimonial bond until the invalidity would be incontestably established. Through this officer a check was placed on the judge in a matrimonial trial to prevent a hasty and precipitate decision nullifying the contract. Likewise, a check was organized for the parties involved in the contract, lest through fraudulent cooperation, one or the other refuse

[10] Can. 1589, § 2; Can. 655, § 2.

[11] Noval, *o. c.*, n. 141.

to answer the summons to court, give false testimony or have recourse to other deception to obtain a favorable sentence.[12]

The Defender in Sacred Orders Trial. He is also a public official whose duty it is to uphold the validity of an ordination which is contested in the ecclesiastical court. He is a promotor of justice in a specified field of action. This office was instituted through an Instruction of the Sacred Congregation of the Council, issued in the year 1836. The provisions of this instruction, in a general way, forms the basis of the present legislation of the Code in regard to the defender of the bond in a case where the validity of an ordination is questioned.

Canonical Requirements for Offices. In these offices as in other offices of the curia, the Code specifies, lays down explicit regulations as to what persons may be chosen, and the moral and mental qualifications requisite for a candidate:

(1) The one selected for the office of promotor of justice or defender of the bond must be a priest.

(2) As to *moral* fitness, the Code requires that the candidate enjoy the esteem and admiration of honest men. He must possess a good name.

(3) Intellectually, the Code prescribes a knowledge of Canon Law, either a doctor in this science or a good knowledge of the law. Added to this the candidate must be a prudent priest in whom there is a prudently regulated zeal for the virtue of justice.

(4) The promotor of justice in a tribunal of a religious order should be a member of the order, a priest of good name, a canonist, upright and zealous for truth and justice.[13]

Presence Required for Validity of Legal Process. In quoting Canon 1586 at the opening of this chapter and in the paragraphs which followed, the origin and pur-

[12] Noval, *o. c.*, n. 141.

[13] Can. 1589, § 1 and § 2.

pose of instituting the office of promotor was stated. There will arise cases in ecclesiastical procedure in which a contest arises over the validity of a matrimonial contract, and consequent obligations, or a contest over the validity of sacred orders and the obligations arising from the reception of this Sacrament. In every such case, the presence of the promotor of justice or the defender of the bond, as the case may demand, is required by the Code.[14] If the judge fails to cite the promotor, the process is null.[15]

The promotor of justice must answer the citation to the court which the judge issues. Should the promotor appear "non citato," his presence is effective and the process is thus rescued from nullity and invalidity.[16]

Having answered the citation, is it necessary that the promotor be present for all the acts and proceedings of the court? Paragraph two of Can. 1587 answers this question in the negative. It is necessary however that the promotor review and examine the acts of the process as drawn up by the appointed notary. Having examined these the promotor or defender, as the case may be, may then, in writing or orally, make any comments and recommendations which the case under consideration demands.[17]

Noval interpreting this Canon, states that, after the promotor has acknowledged the citation he may absent himself from *all* the court sessions, being mindful of his obligations, of course, to carefully examine the record of the process.[18] Noval bases this statement on the prescription of Canon 1680.

Promotor and Defender in a Single Officer. It has already been pointed out that the defender of the bond is simply acting as a promotor of justice in a matrimonial cause or the cause of a disputed ordination. Defending justice and truth when there is an attempt to dissolve

[14] Can. 1586.

[15] Can. 1587, § 1.

[16] Can. 1587.

[17] Can. 1587, § 2.

[18] Noval, *o. c.*, n. 141.

the sacred bond of matrimony, or the sacred obligations of Holy Orders are but two of numerous possible processes where the presence of the promotor of justice may be required. Hence the Code permits and suggests that the promotor and defender may be vested in a single officer in the curia. This admonition is quick to follow, however, "nisi multiplicitas negatiorium et causarum id prohibeat."[19] Should the promotor of justice be called to act in a matrimonial case, in which there is an attempt to annul the bond, the very nature of the case demands the presence of two distinct officers, a *promotor* and a *defender*. The ordinary of the diocese, knowing well the needs of his diocese, will construct this section of his curia according to the needs of his diocese, and at the same time keeping before his mind the will of the Church as expressed in the Code.

The Code leaves it entirely to the judgment of the ordinary as to whether this officer shall be appointed with a certain degree of permanence—"ad universitatem causarum," or merely for a particular and specified cause. These conditions will be specified when the appointment is made, as well as any reservations, limiting the power of these officers which the bishop may deem necessary to make.[20]

Cessation of the Office. If the see of the diocese be vacated, what is the status of the promotor of justice and the defender of the bond? This question is answered in Canon 1590:

§ 1. **Promotor iustitiae et vinculi defensor electi ad universitatem causarum a munere non cessant, sede episcopali vacante, nec a vicario Capitulari possunt removeri; adveniente autem novo Praelato, indigent confirmatione.**

If the appointment was made as permanent, "semel pro semper," the promotor of justice will continue to hold office—"sede vacante." Logically then, if the ap-

[19] Can. 1588, § 1.
[20] Can. 1588, Noval, *o. c.*, n. 146.

pointment was " ad tempus," for example, for a particular cause, when the cause is decided the office ceases ipso facto.

The appointment cannot be recalled by the vicar capitular. If an apostolic Administrator be appointed over the diocese and his appointment is permanent, he may recall the appointment. This right is granted in paragraph two of Canon 1590 and Canon 315. The former law grants the bishop the right to remove the officers we are considering for any just cause. The latter citation regulates the rights and honors which accompany the office of permanent Apostolic Administrator—"iisdem iuribus et honoribus fruitur, iisdemque obligationibus tenetur, ac Episcopus residentialis." [21]

With the advent of the new prelate, the promotor of justice and defender of the bond will need a confirmation of their position in office from him. This is not a new election, but rather an approval of their continuance in the service of the diocesan curia. Hence they will continue in office if they are not removed by an express recall of the appointment. The law imposes the obligation of confirmation on the *ordinary* of the diocese, the obligation of confirming or removing these officers of the curia in the diocese to which he is assigned.[22]

The Notary.

The notary is one who, from a series of notes or signs constructs an authentic report of an event to which he was a witness. A notary in the canonical sense is thus defined by Noval: "est persona publica, creata a publica auctoritate, ut de actis data opera et solemniter coram se gestis, et ab ipso sub forma publici instrumenti, scriptis vel subscriptis, faciat fidem publicam." [23]

The notary, therefore, is to be considered a public person, appointed by one in authority, and his notes or

[21] Can. 315, § 1.
[22] Noval, *o. c.*, n. 148.
[23] Noval, *o. c.*, n. 1-38.

record has more weight than the report of a mere private person acting without authorization.

Notaries, in their legal rating, may be classed as judicial and extra-judicial. The former, or judicial notaries, are appointed to record judicial acts, such as an ecclesiastical trial. The latter, extra-judicial notaries, may be called upon to authenticate other acts or documents such as sale, contracts, wills and similar acts.

History. Both the title and office of the notary can be traced back to the Imperial Court of Rome. In the Codex Theodosianus there were a set of laws and decisions dealing with the notaries of the imperial Court.[24] Notaries or chancellors were used in most of the royal courts of earlier times and likewise in the papal chanceries and the episcopal sees.[25] It is thought by certain writers of history that the seven regional secretaries in the city of Rome were appointed by Pope St. Clement. The special work of these notaries consisted in recording the "acta martyrum."[26]

Eccelsiastical Notaries. Various names have been used in the course of time to indicate this "persona publica," to whom the task was entrusted of constructing authentic public records of legal proceedings in their various phases. Such titles as *scrinarius, tabellio, notarius, actuarius, cancellarius, secretarius,* are quoted by canonical writers. With a more definite terminology in ecclesiastical law, such as we have today, these various terms have come to have a fixed and definite meaning.

The *scrinarius* is now an archivist. The *tabellio* refers to the cursor of letters. The *notarius* is the notary, but his duties are extrajudicial acts. The *actuarius* is the recorder of official reporter of judicial procedure.[27] Though the Code uses the term "notarius," in describ-

[24] Cod. Thed., 6, 16, *De primicerio el notariis.*

[25] Boudinhon—Cath. Ency., *Notaries.*

[26] Wernz, *o. c.,* vol. V., p. 114, note.

[27] Noval, *o. c.,* n. 139.

ing the duty to be performed, it adds, "qui actuarii officio fungatur." [28]

Previous to the Code, the services of the judicial notary, or the actuarius, in ecclesiastical tribunals, were required by the general law. This regulation was made by Pope Innocent III in the Fourth Council of the Lateran in the year 1215. To quote from the Decretals: "De probationibus," (statuit), "ut tam in iudicio ordinario quam extraordinario iudex semper adhibeat aut publicam si potest habere personam, aut duos viros idoneos, qui fideliter universa iudicii acta exscribant." [29] This regulation is reaffirmed in the Code, and the validity of the record of the proceedings is dependent upon the presence and authentic report which must be drawn up in legal form by the actuary.

Notaries in the Code. Canon 1585 directs the judge "antequam causam cognoscere incipiat," to appoint an actuary, a clerk for the recording of the process of the trial. This clerk, the Code prescribes, is to be selected from the number of lawfully constituted notaries, who are to be appointed by the ordinary of the diocese, following the regulations of Canon 373. Should the bishop designate a clerk for the trial, the judge will recognize the appointment and proceed with the hearing of the trial.[30]

The Appointment of Notary. The following points from the Second Book of the Code may be quoted here in the consideration of this topic.

(1) The bishop is empowered to appoint the notaries in his diocese. The acts and records subsequently drawn up by these notaries are to be regarded as public and authentic.[31]

(2) At the time of the appointment or later the ordi-

[28] Can. 1585.

[29] C. 11, X, *De probationibus*, II, 19.

[30] Can. 1585, § 2.

[31] Can. 373, § 1.

nary is free to make whatever limitations he chooses as to the nature of the notaries' service. He may appoint as judicial, extrajudicial, or merely for certain definite and determined legal acts.[32]

(3) If there be a scarcity of clerics in the diocese, the bishop may appoint laymen to this office. However, in "criminalibus clericorum" the actuary should be a priest.[33]

(4) The notaries must be men of good name and above all suspicion.[34]

(5) The length of the term of office of a notary is entirely dependent upon the will of the one who makes the appointment. Hence, constituted by the ordinary of the diocese, they may be removed or suspended from office by the ordinary or successor or superior. The vicar capitular can act in the matter only with the consent of the Cathedral Chapter.[35]

The Duties of a Notary. It is the duty of a notary to prepare a written report of the court proceedings, including the acts, citations, decisions and the sentences of the court. The written report of the proceedings in the court must be given with detailed information as to the place, day, month and year. To those who lawfully make the request "servatis servandis," the notary will show a copy of his report. The official capacity to act as clerk or in general as a notary is confined to the territorial limits of the diocese of the ordinary who appointed him.[36]

Cursors and Apparitors.

The cursor and apparitor are also listed among the officers in the judicial department of the diocesan curia. Canon 1591 states the nature of the duty which is proper to these offices: " ad acta iudicalia intimandae, nisi alia sit probata tribunalis consuetudo"; concerning the apparitores the same Canon states: "item apparitores ad

[32] Can. 373, § 2.
[33] Can. 373, § 3.
[34] Can. 373, § 4.
[35] Can. 373, § 4.
[36] Can. 374.

sententias ac decreta iudicist, eo commitente, exsecutioni mandanda." Before giving an interpretation of this Canon a few words on the history will be given.

History. In Roman Law the legal title of " viator," "apparitor," and "nuncius" is applied to this office.[37] These officers performed the menial tasks, such as carrying messages and reports for the magistrates and senators. Livy refers to the "viatores" attached to the service of a particular magistrate. The magistrate might order the viator to execute a certain sentence, thus he acted in the capacity of a lector.

In the Gallic law the cursor was merely a messenger in the service of a judge. At least this was the position before the Revolution. After the French Revolution, the cursor acted with greater power, conducted the execution of a sentence independent of a judicial sentence or an order from the judge.

According to the German law, the cursor and apparitor exercise the powers of jurisdiction, since according to that Code the execution of a sentence implies jurisdiction.

In Italian and modern French law these officers probably have only administrative powers. It seems to be the opinion of jurists that the execution of a sentence does not imply the power of jurisdiction.

Cursor in Canon Law. The distinction between the office of the cursor and that of the apparitor seems to be very slight. They act according to the order which comes to them from the judge. This order may be the conveying of judicial information, a message from the court to one of the parties in litigation. The judge may commit the execution of a sentence, which he has passed, to the apparitor. Hence the apparitor is to be considered as the material agent who accomplishes the will of the judge. The phrase "ad sententia . . . exsecutioni mandanda" is to be interpreted in the light of the canons

[37] Smith, *Dict. of Antiq.* cf. "viator."

comprised under the seventeenth title of Book Four of the Code. This title deals expressly with the execution of a judicial sentence. According to the norms of this section, "*Sententiam executioni mandare debet per se vel per alium Ordinarium loci in quo sententia primi gradus lata est.*"[39] The judge is the true and proper "exsecutor" of the judicial sentence.

One and the same person may be commissioned to act as cursor and apparitor.[39] Laymen may be selected for this office unless the case be such that prudence requires the services of an ecclesiastic. The judge of the cause will determine this point according to the nature of the cause. Furthermore, he may even dispense with the services of these messengers in the court if there exist—"alia probata tribunalis consuetudo." Such an approved custom or practise would be the use of special or registered mail for the sending out of messages and notifications from the court. A registered letter is quite safe, and its use well enough established to replace the services of the cursor.

The Oath of Fidelity. The Code requires that the bishop make the appointments, to the various offices which have been considered in the preceding pages, in writing. Before proceeding to the duties of their respective offices, the officers of the curia make a promise of fidelity in serving the bishop and the interests of the diocese. They will furthermore promise to observe the norms of the law in fulfilling their various duties. The bishop will also exact of the officers in the curia that they hold all official matters as secrets to be kept within the limits of the official household.[40]

[38] Can. 1920.
[39] Can. 1591, § 2.
[40] Can. 364.

BIBLIOGRAPHY.

Acta Sanctae Sedis, Romae, 1865-1908.

Codex Iuris Canonici, Neo Eboraci, 1918.

Collectanea S. Cong. de Prop. Fide, Romae, 1918.

Corpus Iuris Canonici, Richter-Friedburg, Lipsiae, 1922.

Benedict XIV, Tom. II, De Synodo Diocesano.

Corpus Iuris Civilis, Paul Kreuger, Berlin, 1895.

REFERENCES.

Analecta Juris Pontificii, Paris, 1858.

Bouix, D., *Tractatus de Judiciis,* Paris, 1883.

Bouix, D., *Institutiones Juris Canonici,* Paris, 1859.

Burke, Thomas J., *Competence in Ecclesiastical Tribunals,* Washington, 1922.

Duargin, Edward Vincent, *Reserved Censures,* Washington, 1924.

Devoti, Joannis, *Institutiones Canonicae,* Leodii, 1883.

Fournier, l'Abbé Edouard, *Les Origines du Vicaire Général,* Paris, 1922.

Hinschius, Dr. Paul, *System des Katholischen Kirchenrechts,* Berlin, 1878.

Lega, Cardinal, *De Judiciis Ecclesiasticis,* Roma, 1890.

Leurenius, R. Petrus, *Forum Beneficiale,* Venetiis, 1752.

Chelodi, Joannes, *Jus Poenale,* Tridenti, 1920.

Noval, Juseph, O. P., *Comm. Codicis Juris Canonici,* Roma, 1920.

Maroto, Philippo, *Institutiones Iuris Canonici,* Roma, 1919.

Ojetti, Bendetto, *De Romana Curia, Roma,* 1910.

Pellegrino, D. Abb. Carolo, *Prasia Vicariorum,* Venetiis, 1706.

Reiffenstuel, *Jus Canonicum Universum.*

Thomassinus, *Vetus et Nova Ecclesia Disciplina,* Roma, 1706.

Trudel, Rev. P., S. S., *Dictionary of Canon Law,* Herder, 1919.

Prümmer, D. M., *Manuale Juris Canonici,* Friburgi Brisgoviae, 1922.

Wernz, Francis X., *Jus Decretalium,* 1924.

Pallavicini, P. Sforza, *Histoire de Concile de Trente,* Montrouge, 1844.

Vermeersch-Creusen, *Epitome Juris Canonici,* Mechlin, 1924.

Smith, William, *Dictionary of Greek and Roman Antiquities,* London, 1875.

Catholic Encyclopedia, 15 vols., New York, 1917.

Schmalzgrueber, *Jus Ecclesiasticum Universum,* Romae, 1843-1845.

UNIVERSITAS CATHOLICA AMERICAE

WASHINGTONII, D. C.

SACRA FACULTAS JURIS CANONICI

1924-1925

No. 26.

CANONES

DEUS LUX MEA

CANONES

QUOS

AD DOCTORATUS GRADUM

IN

IURE CANONICO

Apud Universitatem Catholicam Americae

CONSEQUENDUM

PUBLICE PROPUGNABIT

HENRICUS FRANCISCUS DUGAN

SACERDOS DIOECESIS INDIANAPOLITANAE

IURIS CANONICI LICENTIATUS

HORA X A. M. DIE XVIII, MAII A. D. MCMXXV.

CANONES.

I. De Notione et Divisione Juris Canonici.

II. De Collectionibus Canonum usque ad saeculum IX, presertim Latinis.

III. Collectio Pseudo Isidoriana.

IV. De Decreto Gratiani.

V. De Collectione Decretalium Gregorii IX.

VI. De Origine et Editione Novi Codicis.

Book I.

VII. Canones 8-11. De Promulgatione Legum in Ecclesia.

VIII. Canones 15-16. De Legibus Irritantibus seu Inhabilitantibus.

IX. Canones 17-20. De Interpretatione Legum Ecclesiasticarum.

X. Canones 25-30. De Consuetudine.

XI. Canones 31-34. De Temporibus Supputatione.

XII. Canones 12-14. De Legis Canonicae Subiecto.

Book III.

XIII. Canones 738-744. De Ministro Baptismi.

XIV. Canones 777-779. De Collati Baptismi Adnotatione et Probatione.

XV. Canones 814-819. De Missae Ritibus et Ceremoniis.

XVI. Canones 820-823. De Tempore et Loco Missae Celebrandae.

XVII. Canones 853-857. De Subiecto Sacrae Communionis.

XVIII. Canones 858-866. De Subiecto Sacrae Communionis.

XIX. Canones 867-869. De Tempore et Loco quo Sacra Communio Distribui Potest.

XX. Canones 871-874. De Ministro Sacramenti Poenitentiae.

XXI. Canon 883. De Potestae Audiendi Confessionum pro Sacerdotibus in Maritimo Itinere.

XXII. Canon 884. De Absolutione Complicis in Peccato Turpi.

XXIII. Canones 1043-1044. De Potestate Dispensandi ab Impedimentis Matrimonialibus Urgente Mortis Periculo.

XXIV. Canon 1045. De Potestate Dispensandi ab Impedimentis Detectis cum Omnia Parata Sunt ad Nuptias.

BOOKS IV-V.

XXV. Canones 2195-2198. De Natura Delicti eiusque Divisione.

XXVI. Canones 2199-2207. De Imputabilitate Delicti.

XXVII. Canones 2214-2219. De Natura Poenae Ecclesiasticae.

XXVIII. Canones 2257-2267. De Excommunicatione.

XXIX. Canones 2278-2285. De Suspensione.

XXX. Canones 1556-1558. De Foro Competenti.

XXXI. Canones 1552-1555. De Judiciis.

XXXII. Canones 363-365. De Curia Diocesana.

XXXIII. Canones 361-367. De Vicario Generali.

XXXIV. Canones 1580-1584. De Auditoribus et Relatoribus.

XXXV. Canones 1596-1590. De Promotore Justitiae et Defensore Vinculi.

XXXVI. Canones 1572-1574. De Judice.

ROMAN LAW.

XXXVII. The Three Grand Periods of Roman Law and some of the General Principles of Roman Law.

XXXVIII. The Various Books of the Corpus Iuris Civilis considered as to Source and Content.

XXXIX. Personality Defined and the Essential Conditions for Personality in Roman Law.

XL. The Commencement and End of Personality.

XLI. The Modes of Enslavement.

XLII. The Release of a Slave.

XLIII. Roman Conception of Marriage.

XLIV. Matrimonial Impediments in Roman Law.

XLV. Divorce in Roman Law.

XLVI. The Paternal Power.

XLVII. Tutorship.

XLVIII. Curatorship.

INTERNATIONAL LAW.

XLIX. The Nature and Origin of International Law.

L. The Fundamental Principles of International Law.

LI. The Non-Territorial Property of a State.

LII. Sources of International Law.

LIII. The Diplomatic Agents of a State.

LIV. Piracy.

LV. The Monroe Doctrine.

LVI. Extradition Rights.

LVII. Consular Service for a State.

LVIII. Modes of Setling Disputes Amicably.

LIX. General Rights and Obligations of States.

LX. The Advantages of Leagues and World Courts for States.

Vidit Sacra Facultas:

PHILIPPUS BERNARDINI, S. T. D., J. U. D., *Decanus.*
LUDOVICUS H. MOTRY, S. T. D., J. C. D., *a Secretis.*
VALENTINUS T. SCHAAF, O. F. M., J. C. D.
FRANCESCO LARDONE, S. T. D., J. U. D.
MANOEL DE OLIVIERA LIMA, L. H. B.

Vidit Rector Universitatis:

✠ THOMAS J. SHAHAN, S. T. D.

BIOGRAPHY

The writer of this dissertation, Henry Francis Dugan, was born in Indianapolis, September 30, 1889. His primary education was received in St. Anthony's Parochial School of Indianapolis. He was a student in Manual Training High School in the same city for two years. His academic course was completed at St. Mary's College in Kentucky, under the Resurrectionist Fathers in 1910. He spent six years at St. Meinrad Seminary, St. Meinrad, Indiana, where he was ordained priest in the year 1916. For four years he served as curate at the Church of the Assumption in Evansville, Indiana, and taught in the High School during that time. In 1920 he was appointed to teach Philosophy and History in St. Mary-of-the-Woods College, St. Mary-of-the-Woods, Indiana. In the following year he was made Head of the Department of Economics and Social Science in that College. In the years 1921 and 1922 he attended the Summer Sessions at Columbia University, New York, registering in the School of Economics. In the fall of 1923, he entered the Catholic University of America and registered in the School of Canon Law. In November, 1923, he received the degree of Bachelor of Canon Law, and the degree of Licentiate in Canon Law in June, 1924.

www.ingramcontent.com/pod-product-compliance
Lightning Source LLC
LaVergne TN
LVHW050157080826
844660LV00012B/306

* 9 7 8 0 8 1 3 2 2 2 1 6 5 *